Foundational Skills

Phonics for Pre-Kindergarten

SHELL EDUCATION

Contributing Authors

Jodene Smith, M.S.
Mary Rosenberg, M.A.Ed.
Suzanne I. Barchers, Ed.D.
Chandra Prough, M.A.Ed.
Christine Dugan, M.A.Ed.

Publishing Credits

Robin Erickson, *Production Director;* Lee Aucoin, *Creative Director;*
Timothy J. Bradley, *Illustration Manager*; Sara Johnson, M.S.Ed., *Editorial Director*;
Evelyn Garcia, *Editor;* Grace Alba, *Designer*; Corinne Burton, M.A.Ed., *Publisher*

Standards

Shell Education
5301 Oceanus Drive
Huntington Beach, CA 92649-1030
http://www.shelleducation.com

ISBN 978-1-4258-1094-8

Table of Contents

Developing Foundational Skills in Reading

Foundational Skills: Phonics for Pre-Kindergarten has been written with pre-kindergarteners in mind! The pages in this book provide children practice with some of the foundational skills needed to be successful readers—phonics and word recognition.

There has been much written and said about phonics. All the talk has left questions about what phonics is and whether it should be taught. Simply put, phonics is the relationship between letters and sounds. When a child learns that the letter *s* makes the /s/ sound, that is phonics! Since children need to be able to figure out words in order to read, it is important that they understand the relationship between the letters that are on the page and the sounds the letters make (Chall 1995).

There has been much research to show that phonics needs to be explicitly taught and included in good reading programs. In fact, the National Reading Panel (2000) included phonics as one of the five essential components of reading instruction. The fact is that a large number of words in English do follow patterns and rules. Instruction and practice with phonics gives children an opportunity to develop their understanding of the relationship between letters and sounds. Additionally, researchers have found that phonic awareness is a strong predictor of later reading achievement (Juel 1988; Griffith and Olson 1992; Lomax and McGee 1987; Tunmer and Nesdale 1985).

But not all words can be figured out with phonics (Cook 2004). For example, the words *of* and *the* cannot be sounded out with knowledge of letter and sound relationships. There are several word lists that have been compiled of words that occur in print with high frequency, and many of these words do not follow patterns and rules (Fry and Kress 2006). Children need to know other ways to read or figure out words that they cannot apply phonics to, such as recognizing words by sight or using context. For this reason, practice with frequently occurring grade-level-appropriate sight words is an important component of reading.

This book provides children with many opportunities to practice key skills in both phonics and word recognition. Practicing these skills help build the foundation for successful readers. And although the traditional saying is "practice makes perfect," a better saying for this book is "practice makes successful readers."

Understanding the Standards

The Common Core State Standards were developed through the Common Core State Standards Initiative. The standards have been adopted by many states in an effort to create a clear and consistent framework and to prepare students for higher education and the workforce. The standards were developed as educators worked together to incorporate the most effective models from around the country and globe, to provide teachers and parents with a shared understanding of what students are expected to learn at each grade level, and as a continuum throughout the grades. Whereas previously used state-developed standards showed much diversity in what was covered at each grade level, the consistency of the Common Core State Standards provides educators a common understanding of what should be covered at each grade level and to what depth.

The Common Core State Standards have the following qualities:

- They are aligned with college and work expectations.
- They are clear, understandable, and consistent.
- They include rigorous content and application of knowledge through high-order skills.
- They build upon strengths and lessons of current state standards.
- They are informed by other top-performing countries so that all students are prepared to succeed in our global economy and society.
- They are evidence based.

Students who meet these standards within their K–12 educations should have the skills and knowledge necessary to succeed in their educational careers and beyond.

Getting Started

Practicing the phonics skills targeted in this book gives children the foundation they need to become better readers. It is because you realize this that you have purchased this book! Following are some tips for using this book:

- Set aside a specific time of day to work on the activities found in this book. This will establish consistency.
- Emphasize completing only a couple of pages each time the child works in the book rather than lots of activity pages at one time.
- Keep all practice sessions positive and constructive. If the mood becomes tense, or if you and the child get frustrated, set the activities aside and look for another time for the child to practice.
- Help with instructions, if necessary. If the child is having difficulty understanding what to do, talk through some of the problems with him or her.
- Use the answer key provided on pages 89–95. Once the desired number of pages have been completed, help check the work. If possible, take time to go back and correct any problems missed. Immediately reviewing errors with the help of an adult helps children learn from their mistakes.

Making It Work

Understanding the key features of this book will help you effectively use it as you work with the child to develop and practice reading skills. Following are some features of the book that will help you.

- **Standards-based practice.** The exercises in *Foundational Skills: Phonics for Pre-Kindergarten* are aligned with the Common Core State Standards. Each activity page focuses on a particular concept, skill, or skill set and provides students opportunities to practice and achieve mastery.
- **Clear, easy-to-understand activities.** The exercises in this book are written in a user-friendly style.
- **Stand-alone activity pages.** Each activity is flexible and can be used independently.
- **Concise number of exercises.** The number of exercises on each page is limited to six. Children feel more comfortable and confident in attempting a page when the number of exercises is not overwhelming to them.

The chart below provides suggestions for how to implement the activities.

Preteaching Choose pages with concepts the child has not yet learned. This will take some teaching on your part in order to help the child understand the concept, so be sure you are comfortable and prepared to explain the new concept.	**Reteaching** Use pages related to concepts the child has struggled with in school or while doing homework. If there are any areas or specific standards with which the child may need some additional instruction and practice, use the Standards Correlation Chart on page 9 to help locate pages that will be useful.
Practice Select pages that are consistent with what is being taught in school. By providing additional practice with those reading concepts, you will help the child master them more quickly.	**Review** Choose pages with concepts the child may have learned earlier in the school year. By reviewing previously-taught concepts, the child will benefit from refreshing those skills.

Correlations to Standards

Shell Education is committed to producing educational materials that are research- and standards-based. In this effort, we have correlated all of our products to the academic standards of all 50 United States, the District of Columbia, the Department of Defense Dependent Schools, and all Canadian provinces. We have also correlated to the Common Core State Standards.

How to Find Standards Correlations

To print a customized correlation report of this product for your state, visit our website at **http://www.shelleducation.com** and follow the on-screen directions. If you require assistance in printing correlation reports, please contact Customer Service at 1-877-777-3450.

Purpose and Intent of Standards

Legislation mandates that all states adopt academic standards that identify the skills students will learn in kindergarten through grade twelve. Many states also have standards for pre-K. This same legislation sets requirements to ensure the standards are detailed and comprehensive.

Standards are designed to focus instruction and guide adoption of curricula. Standards are statements that describe the criteria necessary for students to meet specific academic goals. They define the knowledge, skills, and content students should acquire at each level. Standards are also used to develop standardized tests to evaluate students' academic progress. Teachers are required to demonstrate how their lessons meet state standards. State standards are used in the development of all of our products, so educators can be assured they meet the academic requirements of each state.

Common Core State Standards

The lessons in this book are aligned to the Common Core State Standards (CCSS). The standards listed on page 9 support the objectives presented throughout the lessons.

Correlations to Standards

Skill	Pages
Demonstrate basic knowledge of one-to-one letter-sound correspondences by producing the primary sound or many of the most frequent sounds for each consonant.	11, 13–19, 21–27, 29–39, 41–51, 53–62
Isolate and pronounce the initial, medial vowel, and final sounds (phonemes) in three-phoneme (consonant-vowel-consonant) words.	12, 20, 28, 40, 52
Associate the long and short sounds with common spellings (graphemes) for the five major vowels.	63–82

Letter Formation Guide

Name: ______________________ **Date:** ______________

Directions: Trace and write.

Directions: Color the *a*'s.

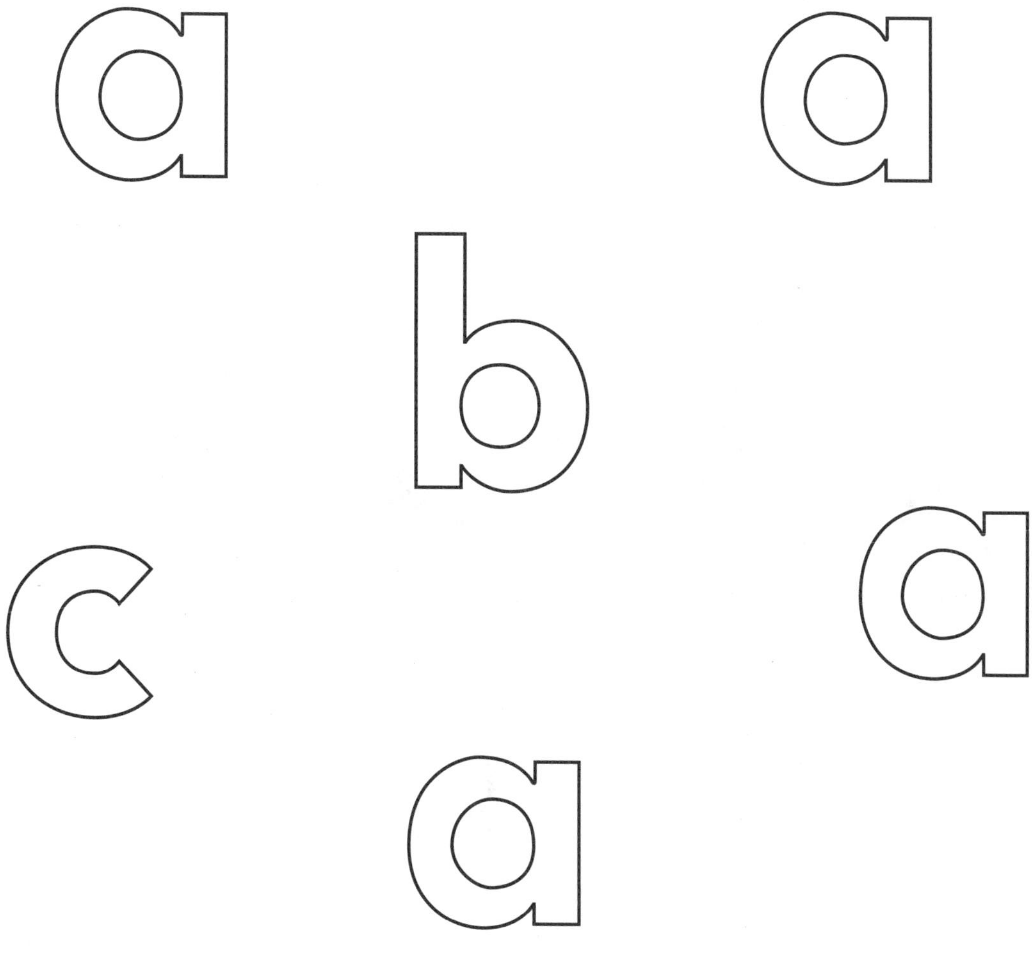

Primary Sound *a*

Name: ______________________________ **Date:** ______________

Directions: Write the missing *a*'s. Color the pictures.

1.

f ___ n

2.

r ___ t

3.

m ___ p

4.

h ___ t

Primary Sound *b*

Name: ______________________________ **Date:** ________________

Directions: Trace and write.

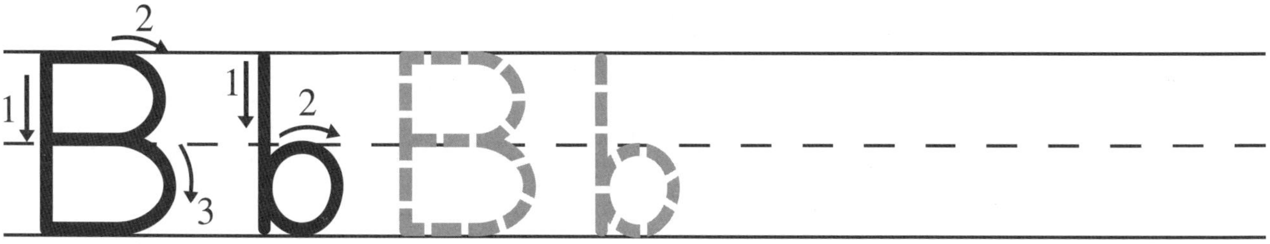

Directions: Color the *b*'s.

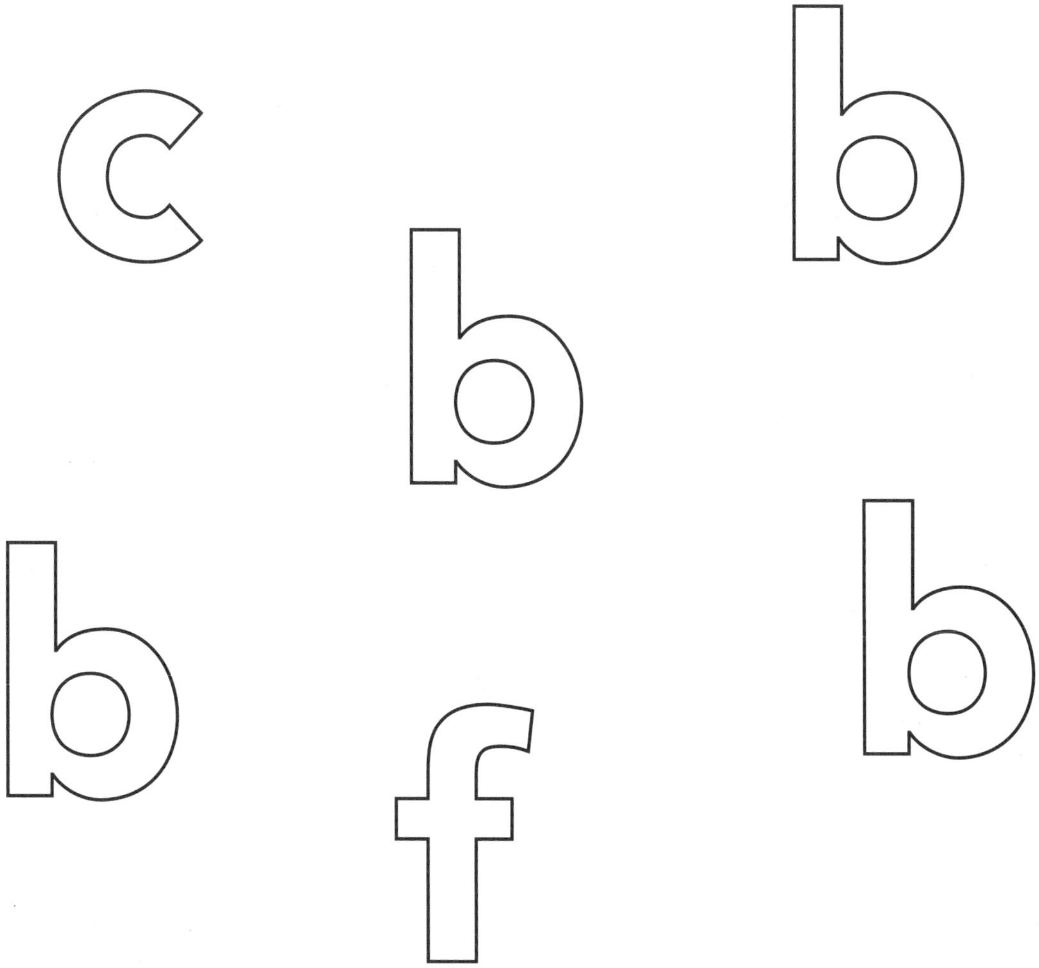

Primary Sound *b*

Name: ______________________ **Date:** ____________

Directions: Write the missing *b*'s. Color the pictures.

1. 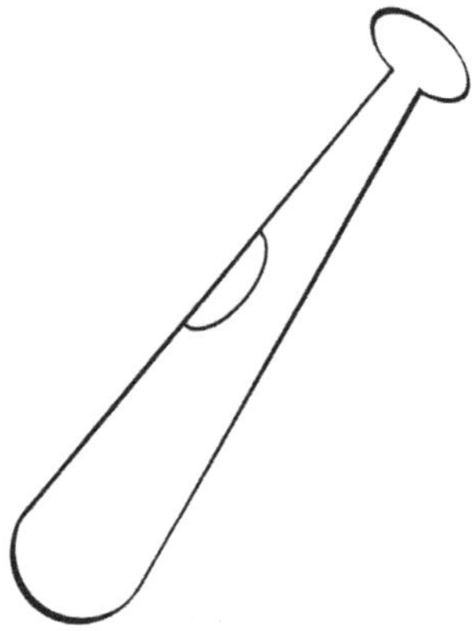 ____at	2. 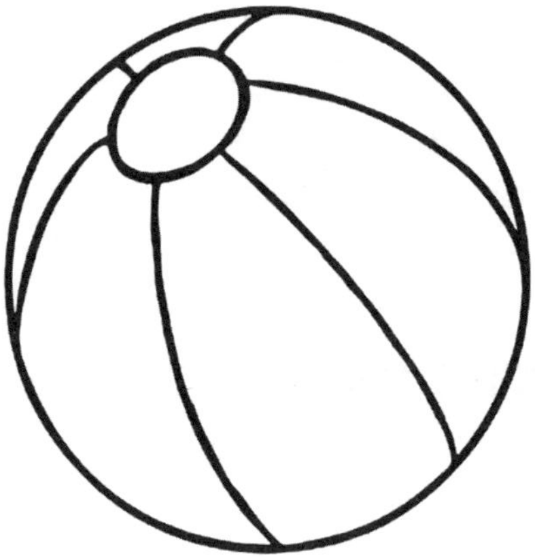 ____all
3.  ____us	4. 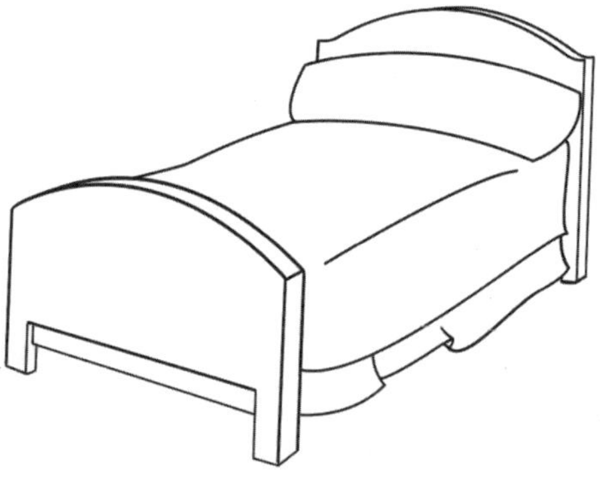 ____ed

Name: ______________________________ **Date:** ________________

Directions: Trace and write.

C c C c

Directions: Color the *c*'s.

c h

b

c c

c

Primary Sound *c*

Name: ______________________________ **Date:** ____________

Directions: Write the missing *c*'s. Color the pictures.

1.  ____at	2.  ____ar
3.  ____ow	4. 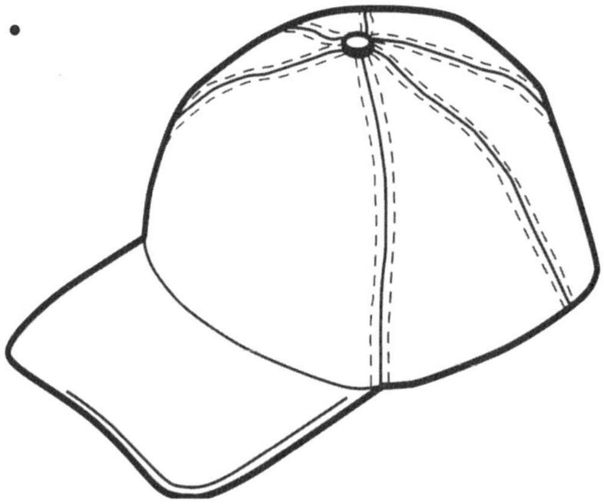 ____ap

Name: ____________________ **Date:** ____________

Directions: Trace and write.

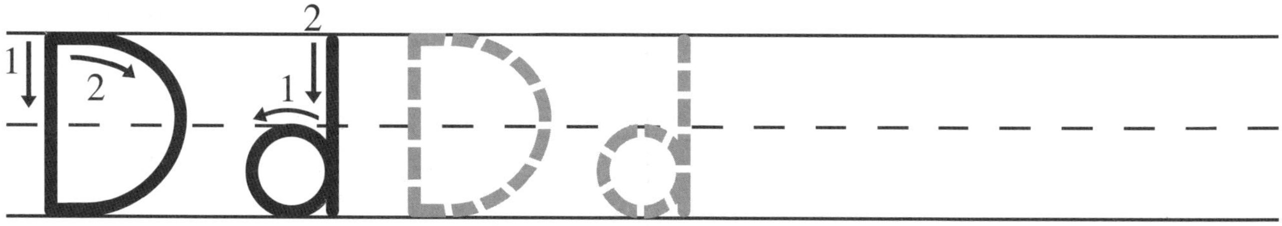

Directions: Color the *d*'s.

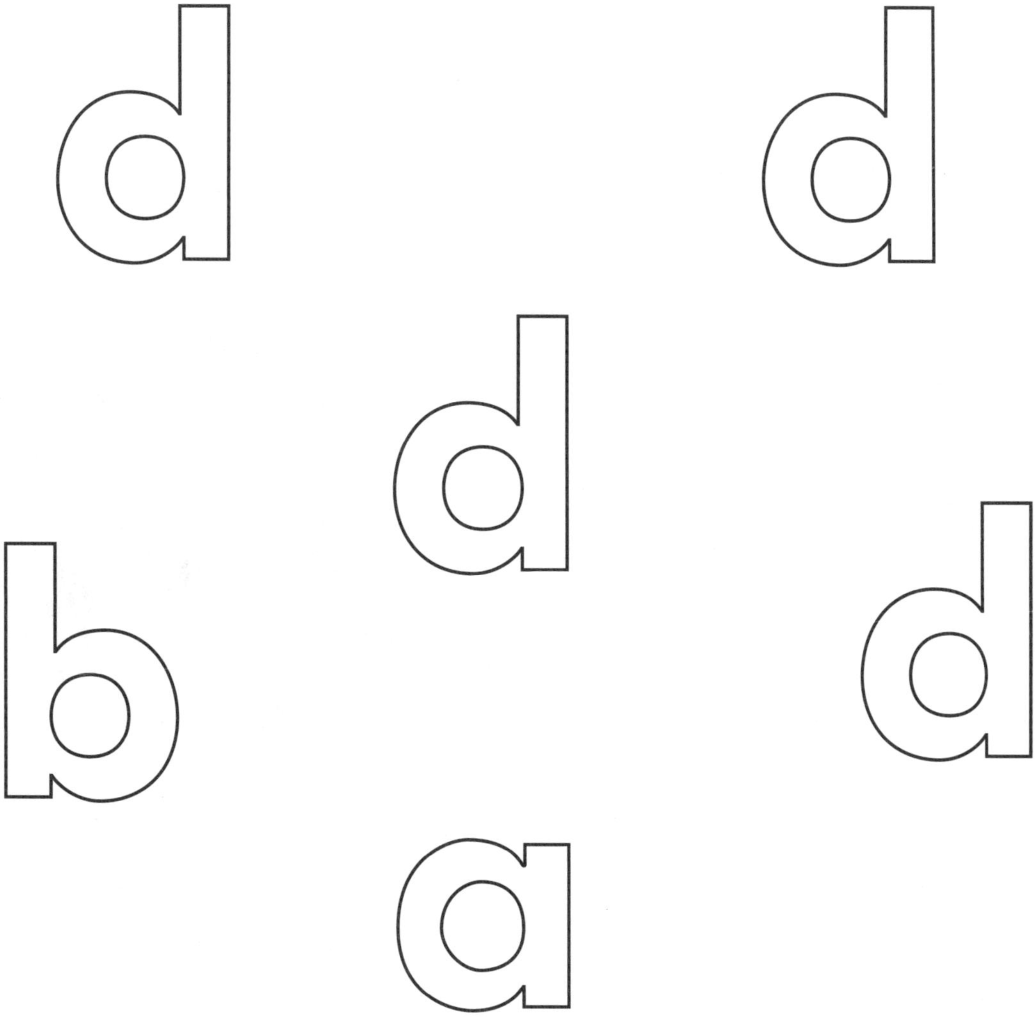

Primary Sound *d*

Name: ______________________ **Date:** ____________

Directions: Write the missing *d*'s. Color the pictures.

1.

____uck

2.

____oll

3.

____og

4.

____rum

Name: ______________________ **Date:** ______________

Directions: Trace and write.

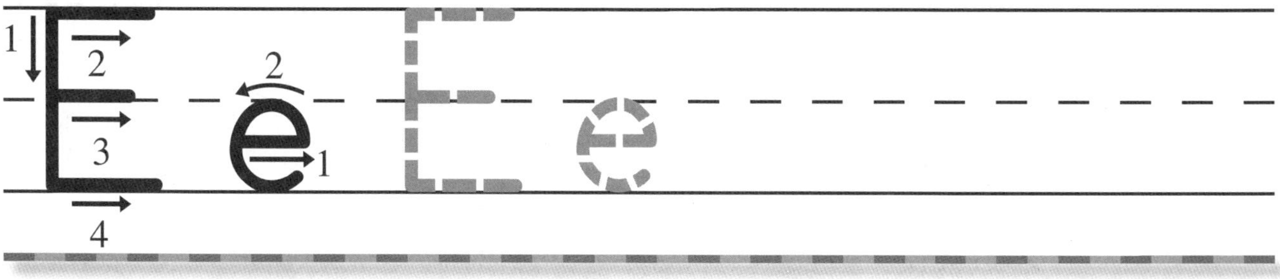

Directions: Color the *e*'s.

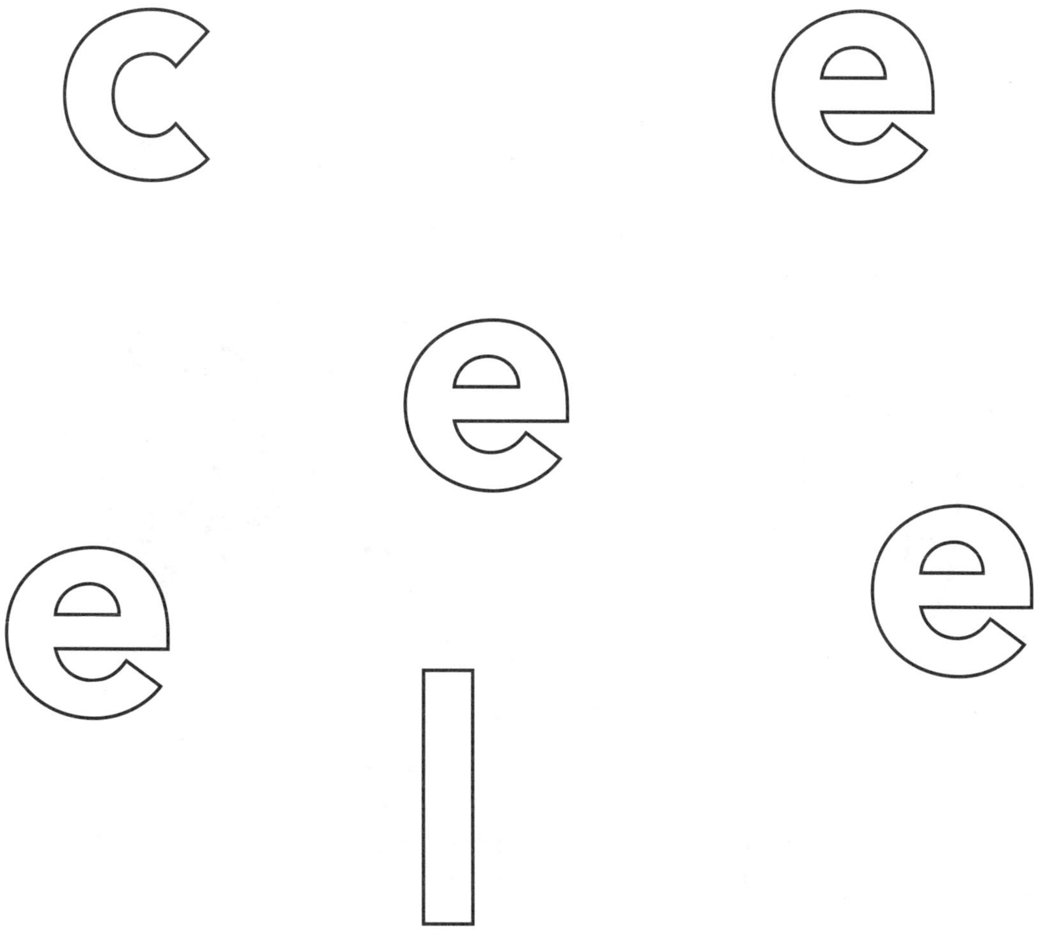

Primary Sound e

Name: ______________________________ **Date:** ____________

Directions: Write the missing *e*'s. Color the pictures.

1.

p ___ n

2.

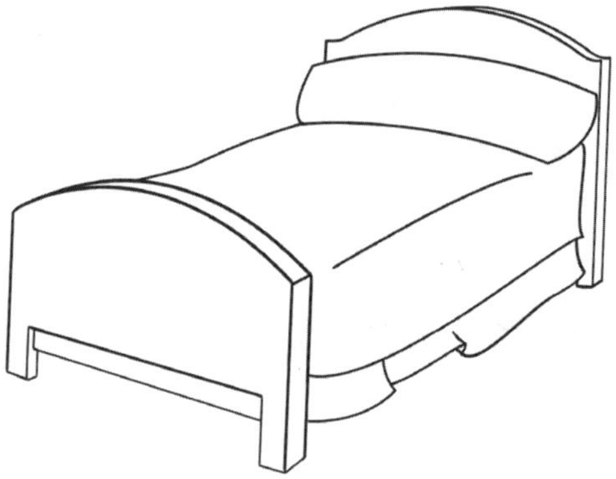

b ___ d

3.

t ___ n

4.

n ___ t

Primary Sound *f*

Name: ______________________ **Date:** ______________

Directions: Trace and write.

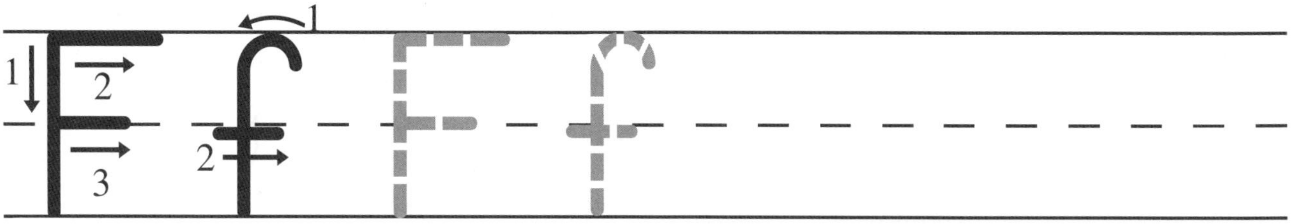

Directions: Color the *f*'s.

Primary Sound *f*

Name: ______________________ **Date:** ____________

Directions: Write the missing *f*'s. Color the pictures.

1.  ___ork	2.  ___an
3.  ___ox	4.  ___rog

Name: ______________________ **Date:** ____________

Directions: Trace and write.

Directions: Color the *g*'s.

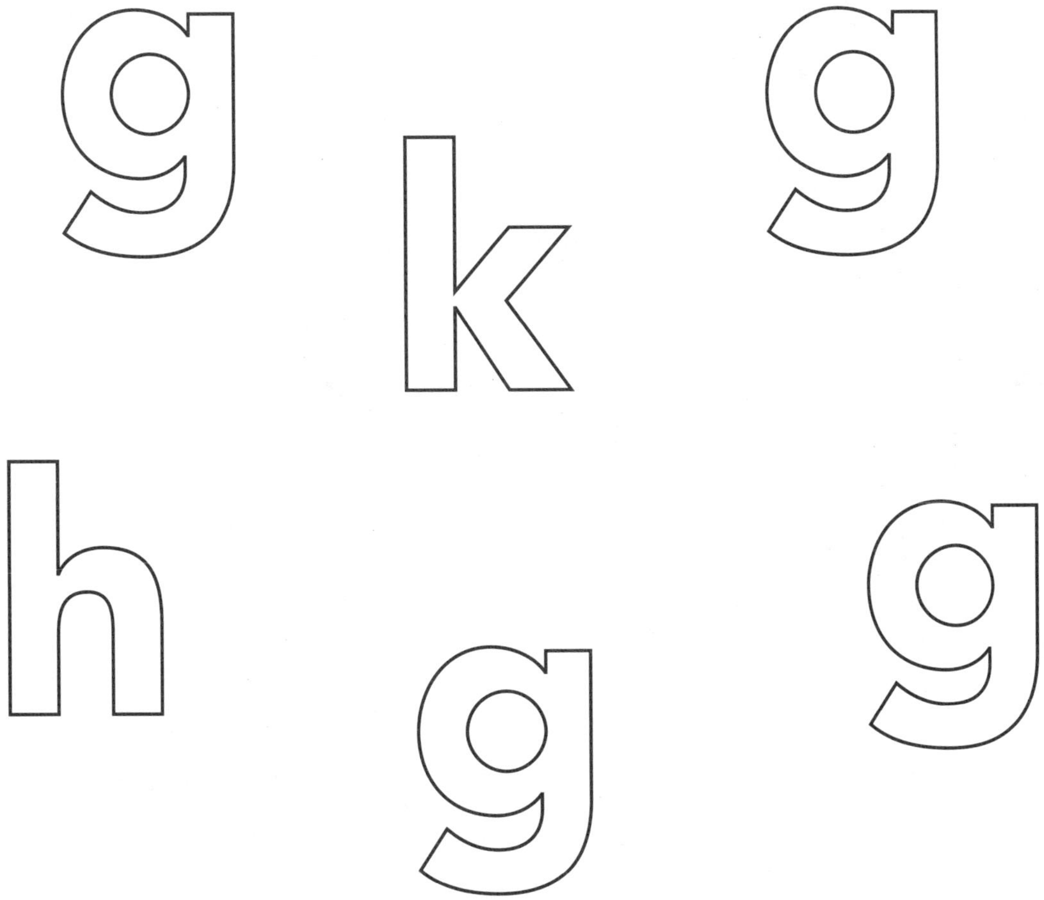

Primary Sound *g*

Name: ______________________________ **Date:** ______________

Directions: Write the missing *g*'s. Color the pictures.

1.  ___ift	2. 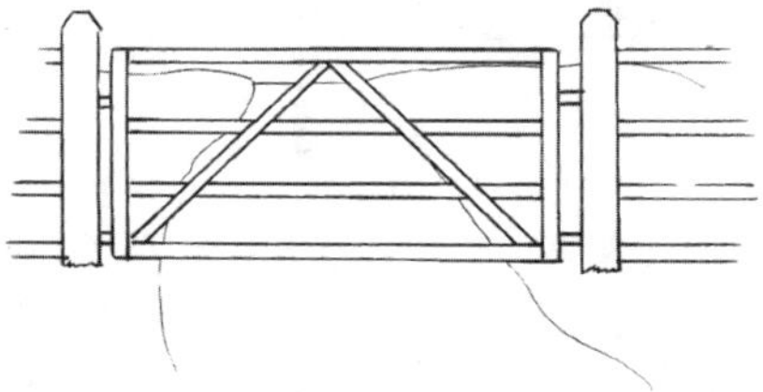 ___ate
3.  ___irl	4.  ___oat

Primary Sound *h*

Name: ______________________________ **Date:** ________________

Directions: Trace and write.

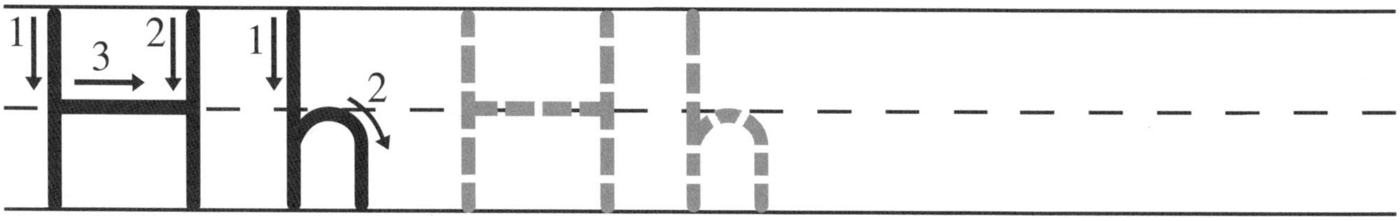

Directions: Color the *h*'s.

c h

h

h h

l

Primary Sound *h*

Name: ______________________________ **Date:** ______________

Directions: Write the missing *h*'s. Color the pictures.

1.

___and

2.

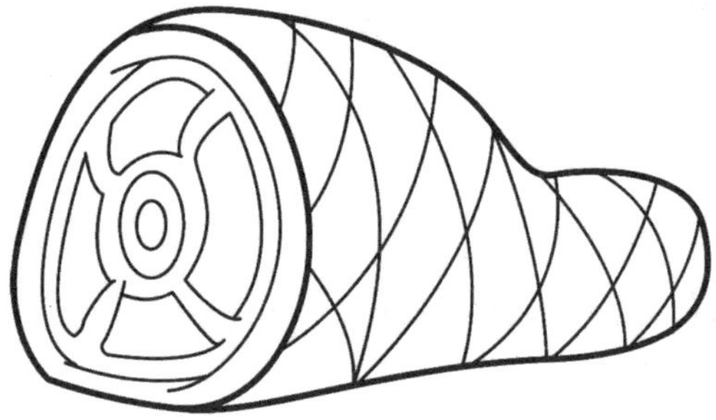

___am

3.

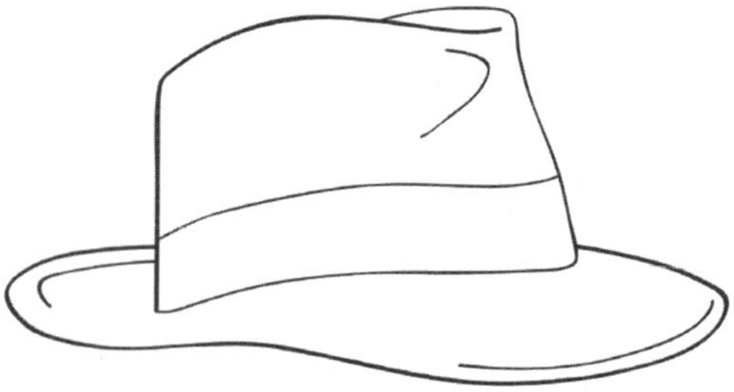

___at

4.

___en

Primary Sound *i*

Name: ______________________________ **Date:** ________________

Directions: Trace and write.

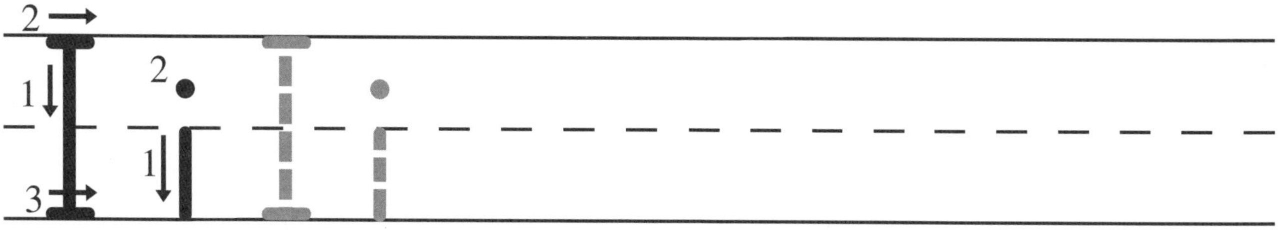

Directions: Color the *i*'s.

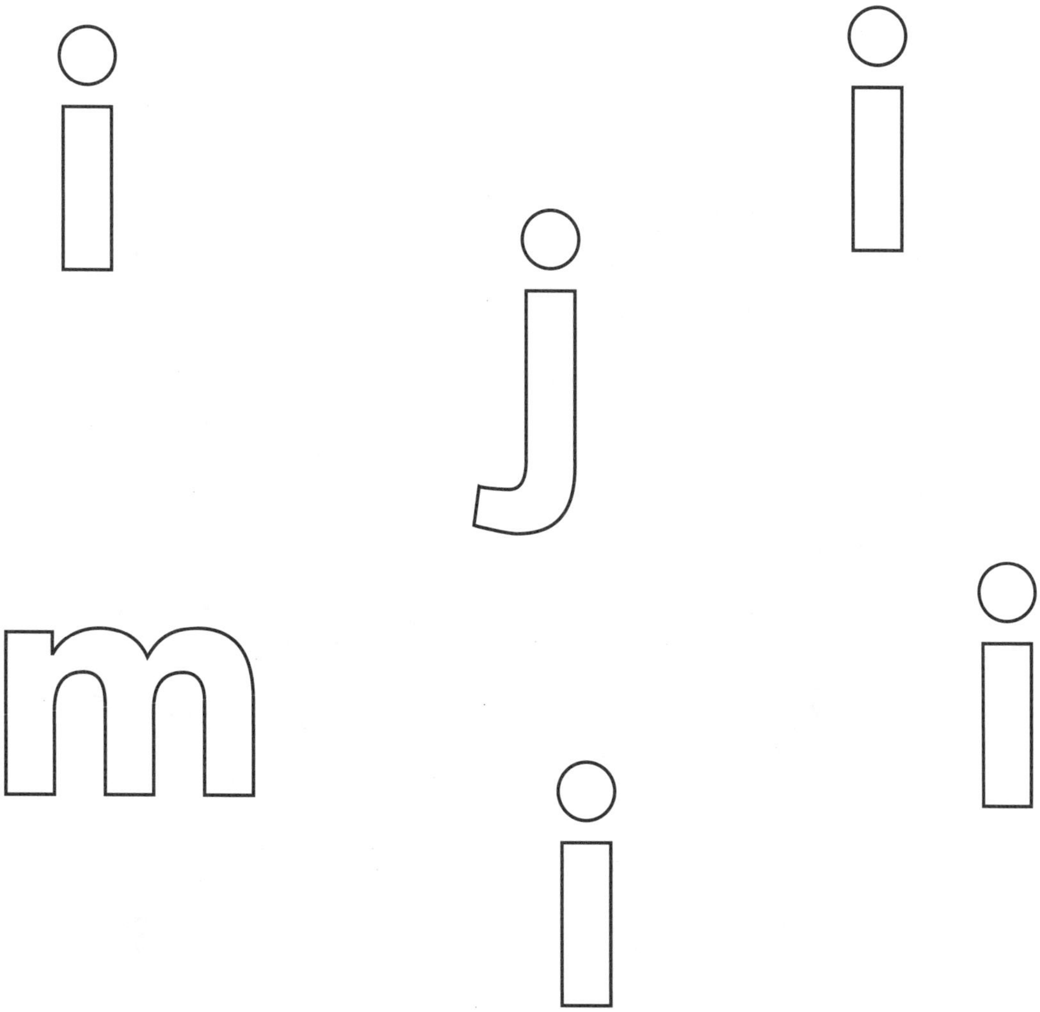

Primary Sound *i*

Name: ______________________ **Date:** ____________

Directions: Write the missing *i*'s. Color the pictures.

1.

w ___ g

2.

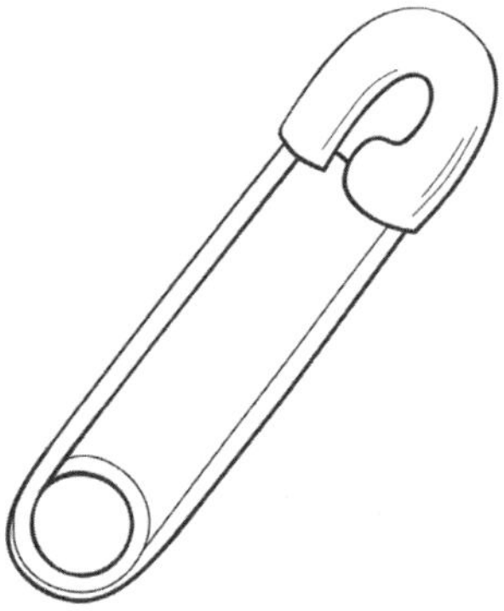

p ___ n

3.

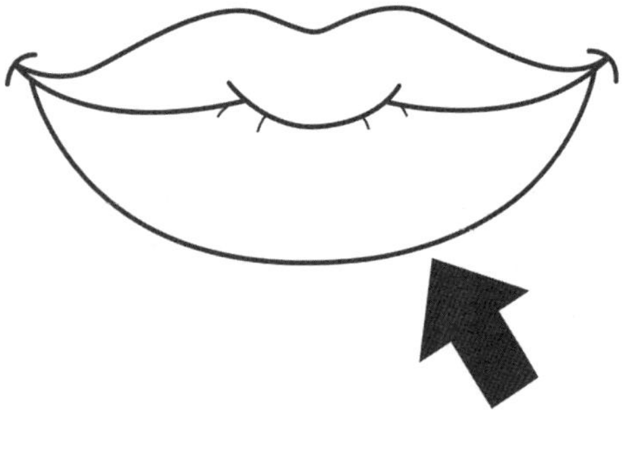

l ___ p

4.

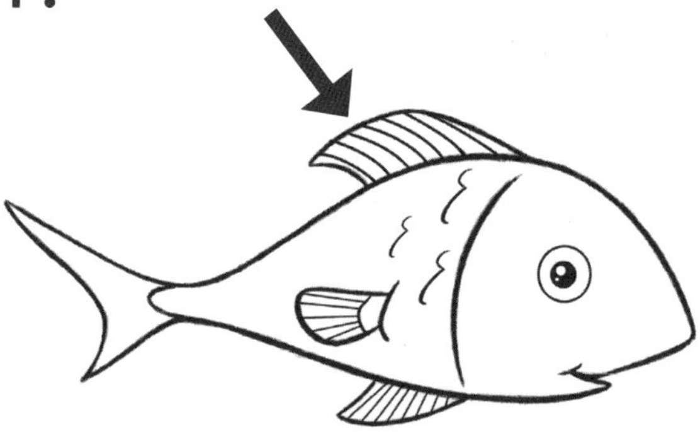

f ___ n

Primary Sound *j*

Name: ______________________ **Date:** ______________

Directions: Trace and write.

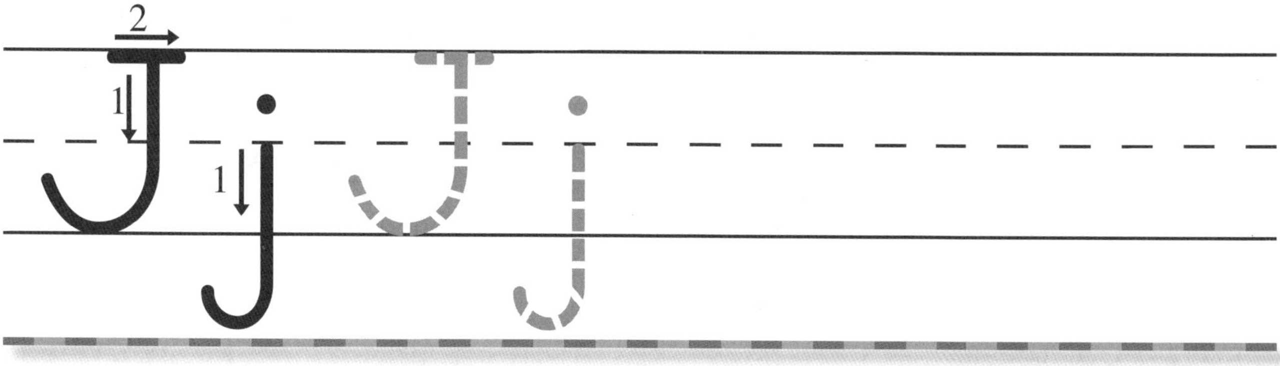

Directions: Color the *j*'s.

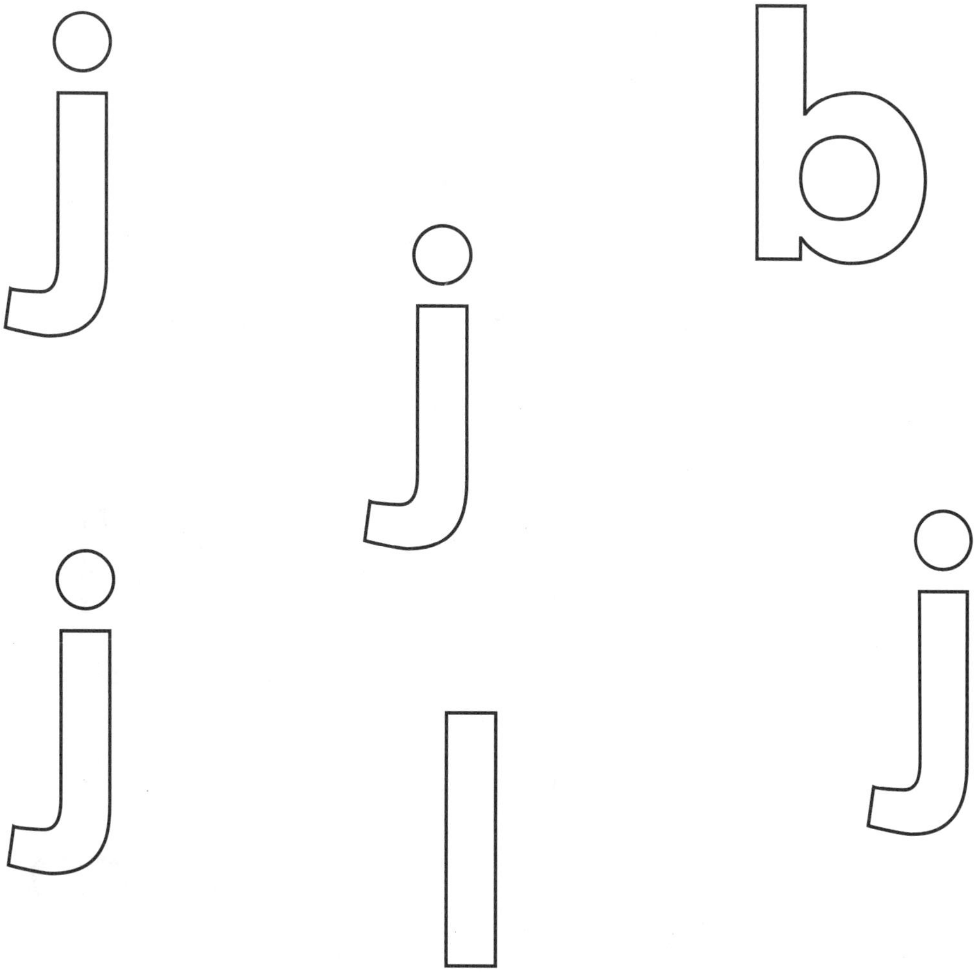

Primary Sound *j*

Name: ______________________ **Date:** ____________

Directions: Write the missing *j*'s. Color the pictures.

1.

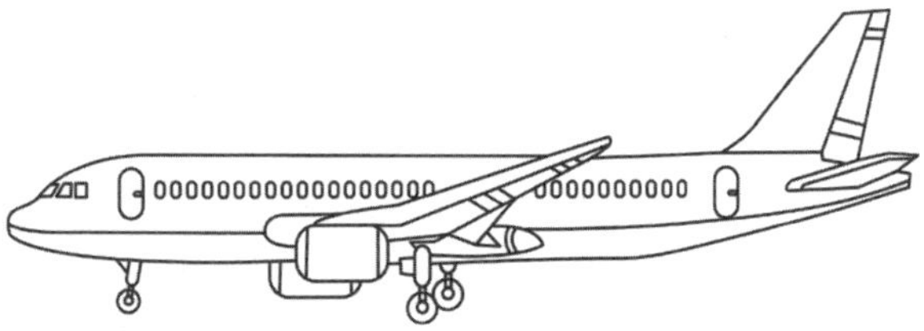

___et

2.

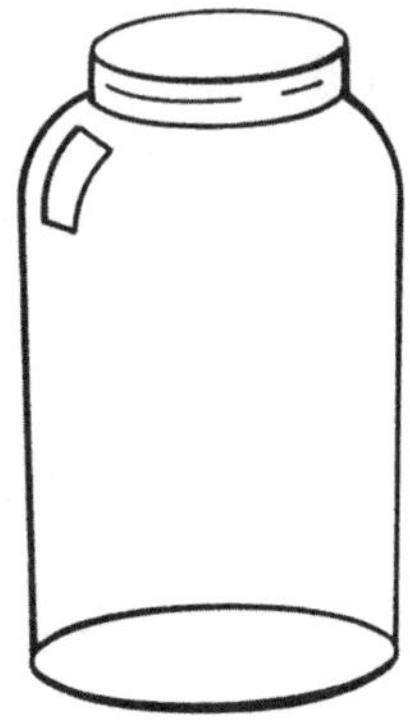

___ar

3.

___ug

4.

___am

Name: ______________________________ **Date:** ________________

Directions: Trace and write.

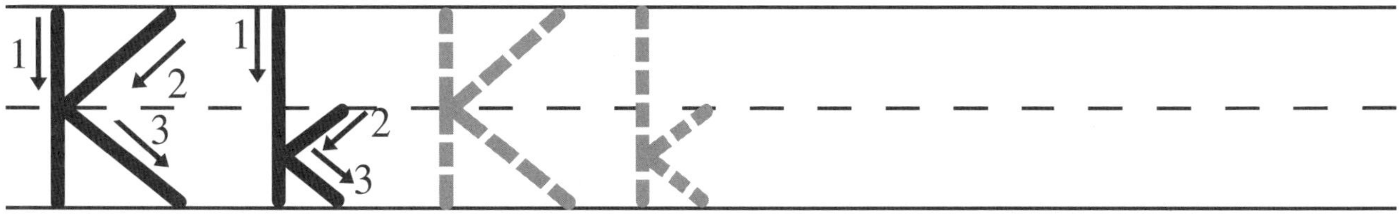

Directions: Color the *k*'s.

k d

k

f k

k

Primary Sound *k*

Name: ______________________ **Date:** ____________

Directions: Write the missing *k*'s. Color the pictures.

1.

_____ey

2.

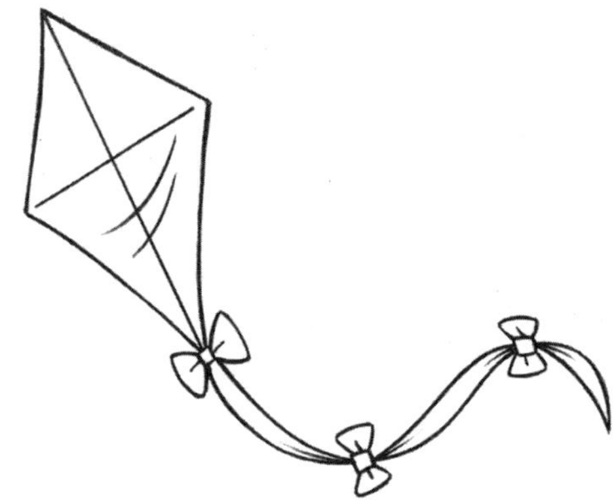

_____ite

3.

_____ing

4.

_____oala

Name: ____________________________ **Date:** ________________

Directions: Trace and write.

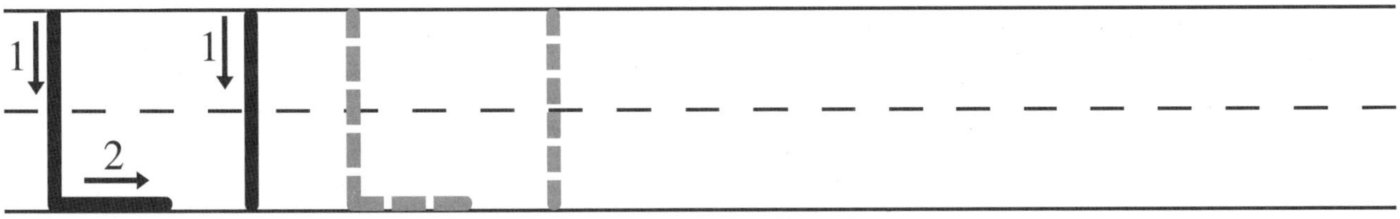

Directions: Color the *l*'s.

Primary Sound *l*

Name: ______________________________ **Date:** ______________

Directions: Write the missing *l*'s. Color the pictures.

1.

___amp

2.

___ion

3.

___ock

4.

___og

Name: ______________________ **Date:** ______________

Directions: Trace and write.

Directions: Color the *m*'s.

m n

m

m m

p

Primary Sound *m*

Name: ______________________________ **Date:** ______________

Directions: Write the missing *m*'s. Color the pictures.

1. 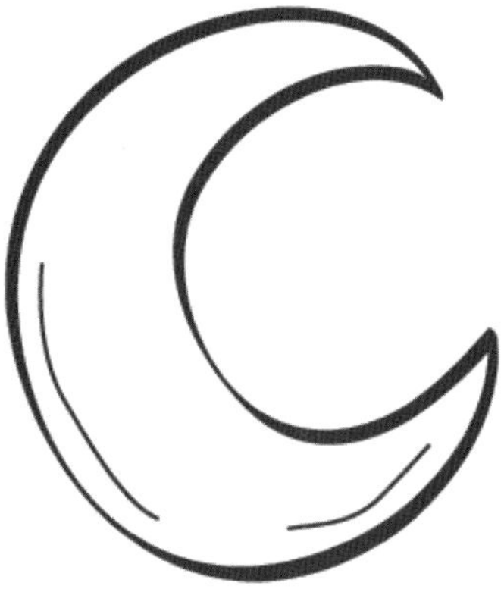 ___oon	2.  ___ap
3.  ___op	4.  ___ug

Primary Sound *n*

Name: ______________________________ **Date:** ________________

Directions: Trace and write.

N n N n

Directions: Color the *n*'s.

s n

s

n n

n

Primary Sound *n*

Name: ______________________________ **Date:** ____________

Directions: Write the missing *n*'s. Color the pictures.

1.

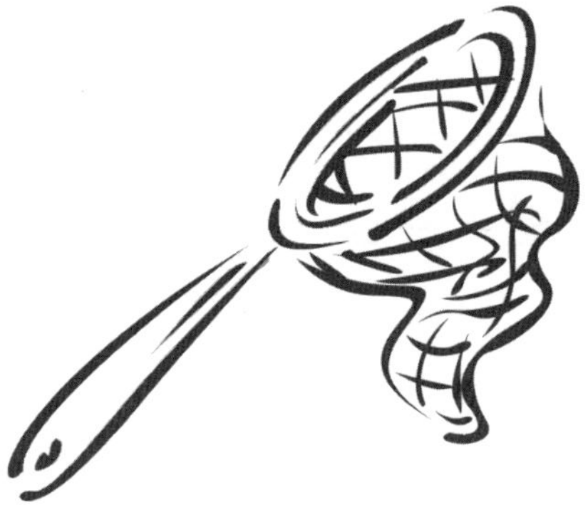

___et

2.

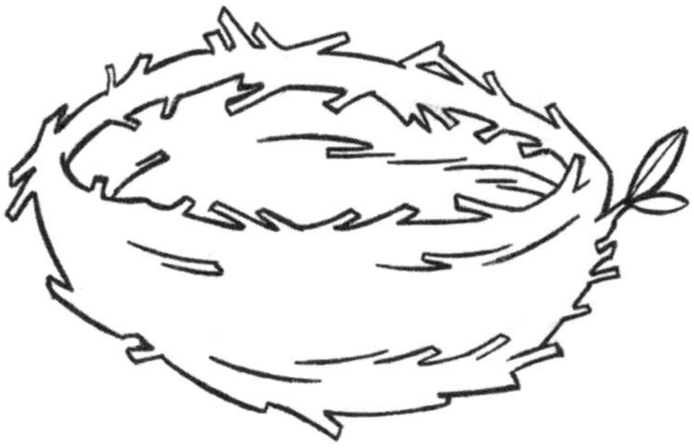

___est

3.

___ose

4.

___ut

Name: ______________________ **Date:** ______________

Directions: Trace and write.

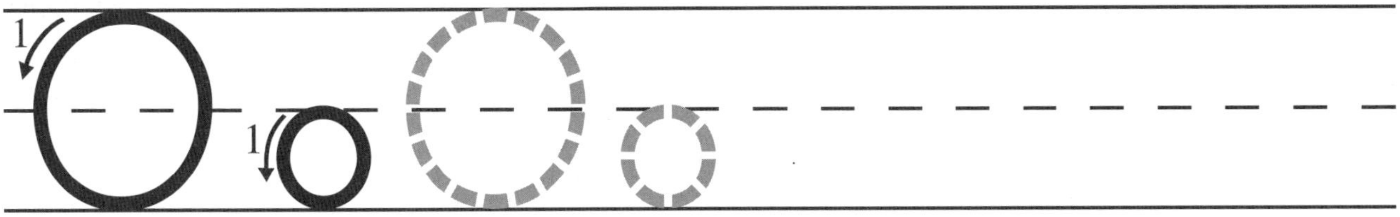

Directions: Color the *o*'s.

o o

p

o v

o

Primary Sound *o*

Name: ______________________ **Date:** ____________

Directions: Write the missing *o*'s. Color the pictures.

1\.

l ___ g

2\.

d ___ t

3\.

c ___ p

4\.

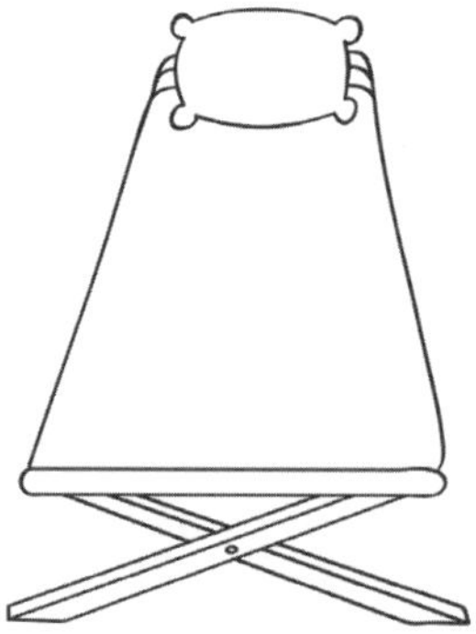

c ___ t

Name: ______________________ **Date:** ______________

Directions: Trace and write.

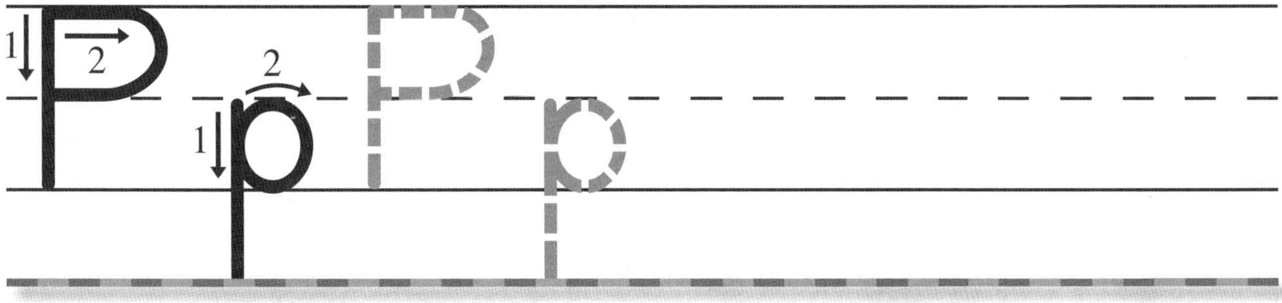

Directions: Color the *p*'s.

Primary Sound *p*

Name: ______________________ **Date:** ____________

Directions: Write the missing *p*'s. Color the pictures.

1.  ___anda	2.  ___an
3. 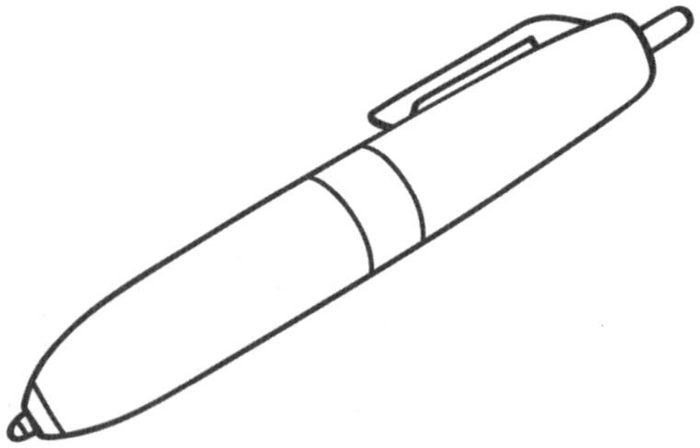 ___en	4.  ___ig

Name: ____________________________ **Date:** ________________

Directions: Trace and write.

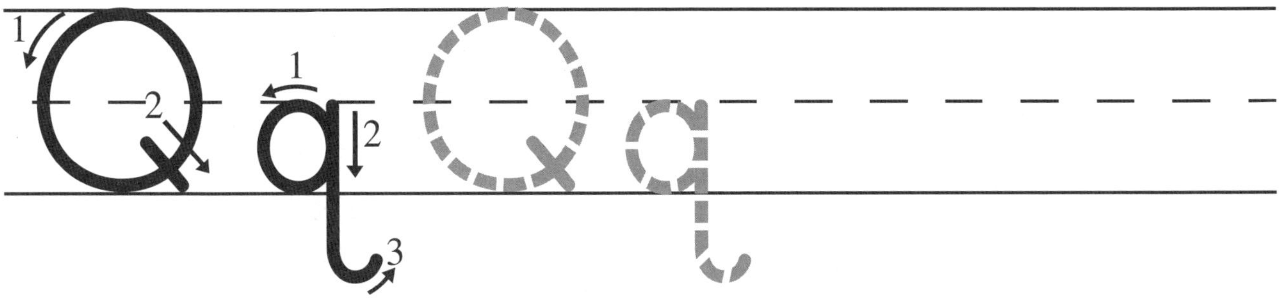

Directions: Color the *q*'s.

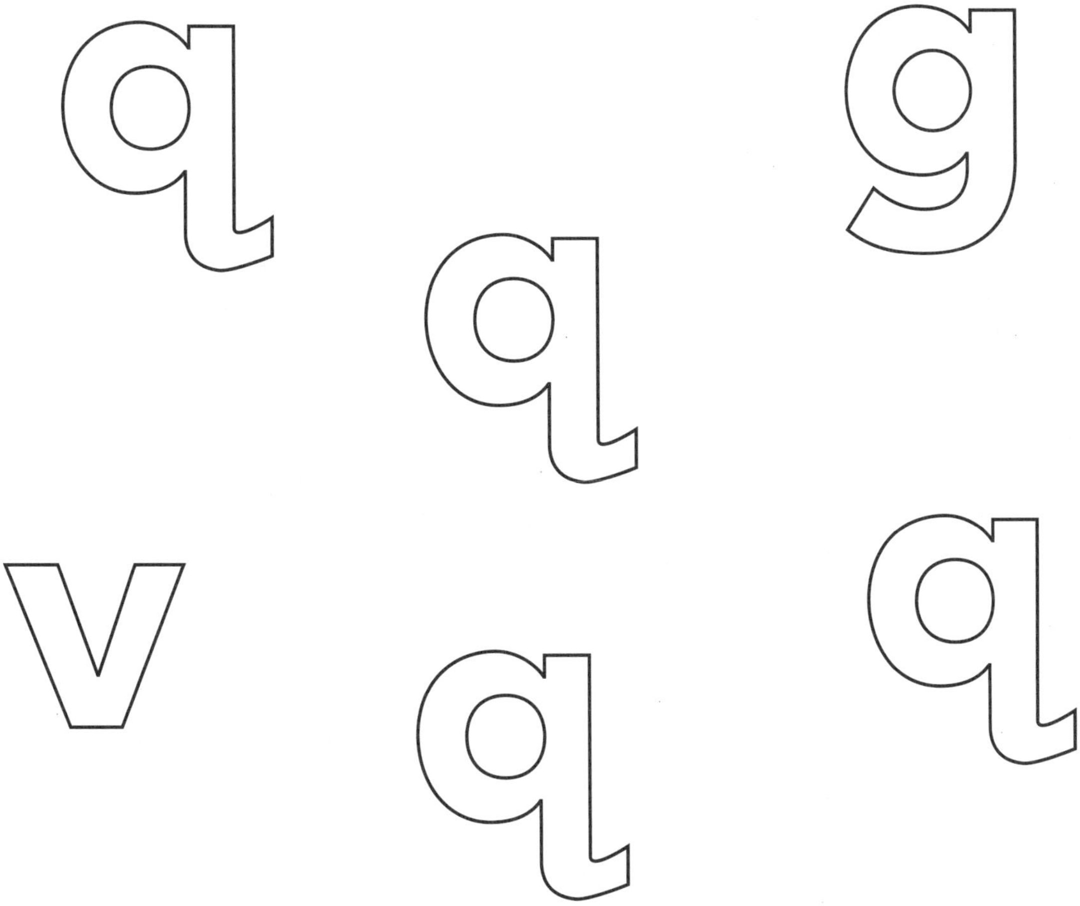

Primary Sound *q*

Name: ______________________________ **Date:** _____________

Directions: Write the missing *q*'s. Color the pictures.

1.  ____uilt	2.  ____ueen
3.  ____uail	4.  ____uarter

Name: ______________________ **Date:** ______________

Directions: Trace and write.

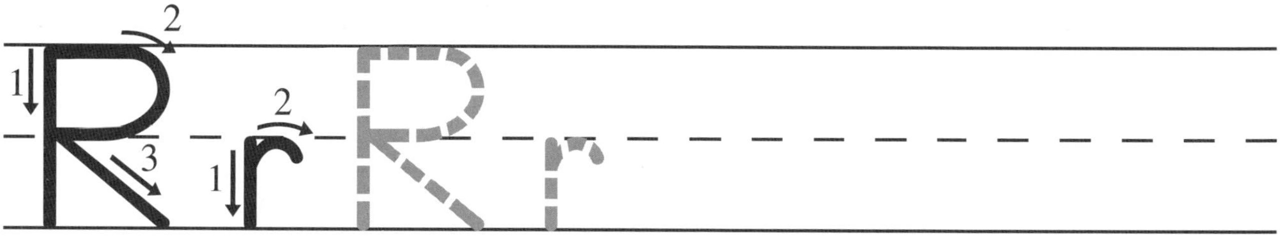

Directions: Color the *r*'s.

r

r

r

m

a

r

Primary Sound *r*

Name: ______________________ **Date:** ____________

Directions: Write the missing *r*'s. Color the pictures.

1.  ___est	2.  ___at
3.  ___ing	4.  ___abbit

Name: ______________________________ **Date:** ________________

Directions: Trace and write.

S s S s

Directions: Color the *s*'s.

s s

n

s w

s

Primary Sound *s*

Name: ______________________________ **Date:** _____________

Directions: Write the missing *s*'s. Color the pictures.

1. 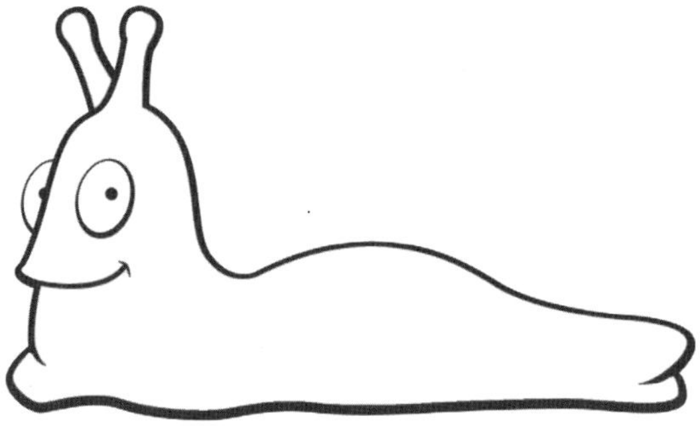 ___lug	2.  ___carf
3. 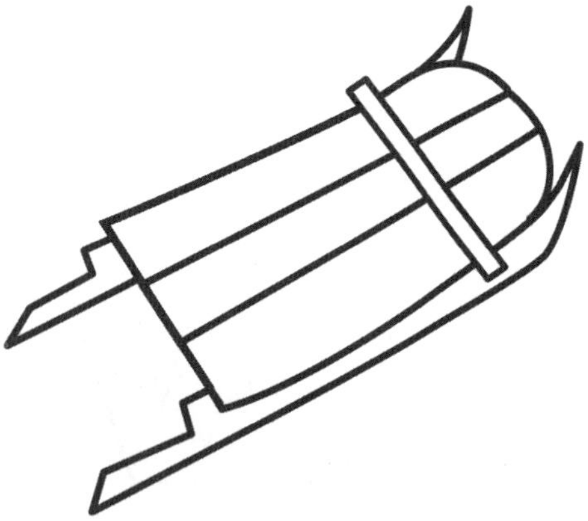 ___led	4. 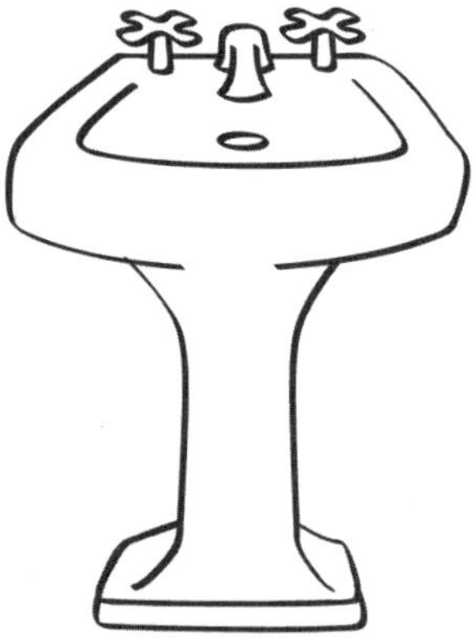 ___ink

Name: ______________________ **Date:** ______________

Directions: Trace and write.

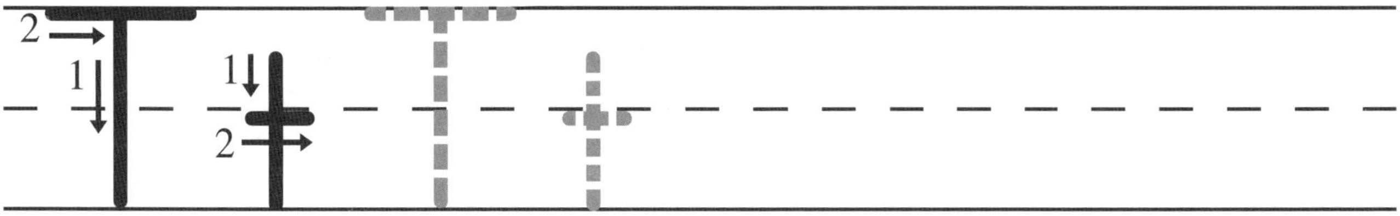

Directions: Color the *t*'s.

Primary Sound *t*

Name: ______________________ **Date:** ____________

Directions: Write the missing *t*'s. Color the pictures.

1.

___able

2.

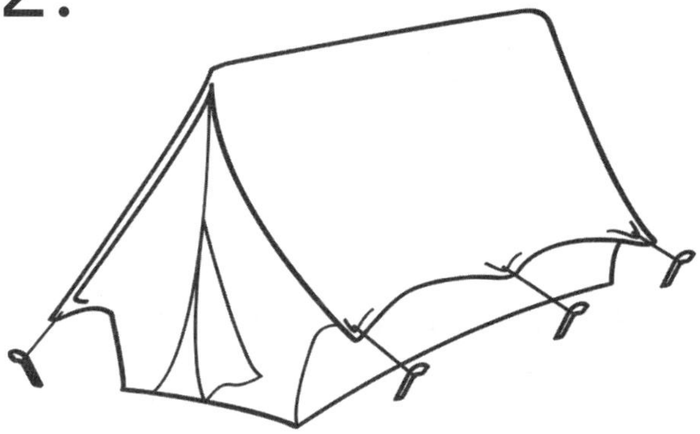

___ent

3.

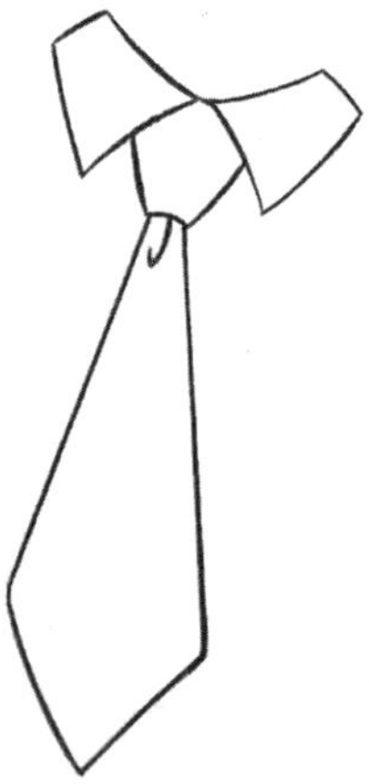

___ie

4.

___ree

Name: ______________________ **Date:** ____________

Directions: Trace and write.

Uu Uu

Directions: Color the *u*'s.

u u

m

u u

p

Primary Sound *u*

Name: ______________________ **Date:** ____________

Directions: Write the missing *u*'s. Color the pictures.

1.

b ___ g

2.

b ___ s

3.

c ___ b

4.

c ___ p

Name: ______________________________ **Date:** ________________

Directions: Trace and write.

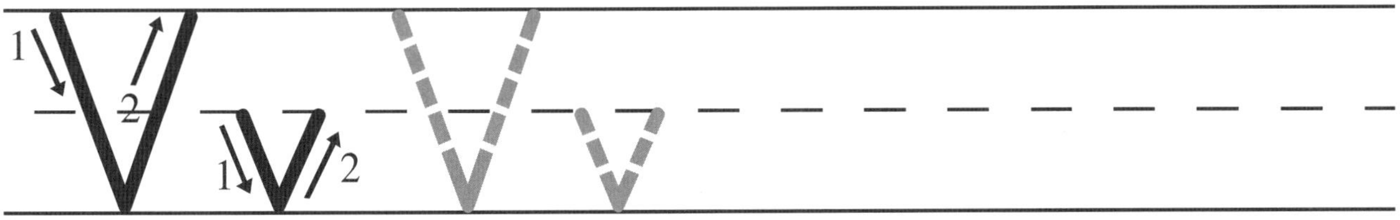

Directions: Color the *v*'s.

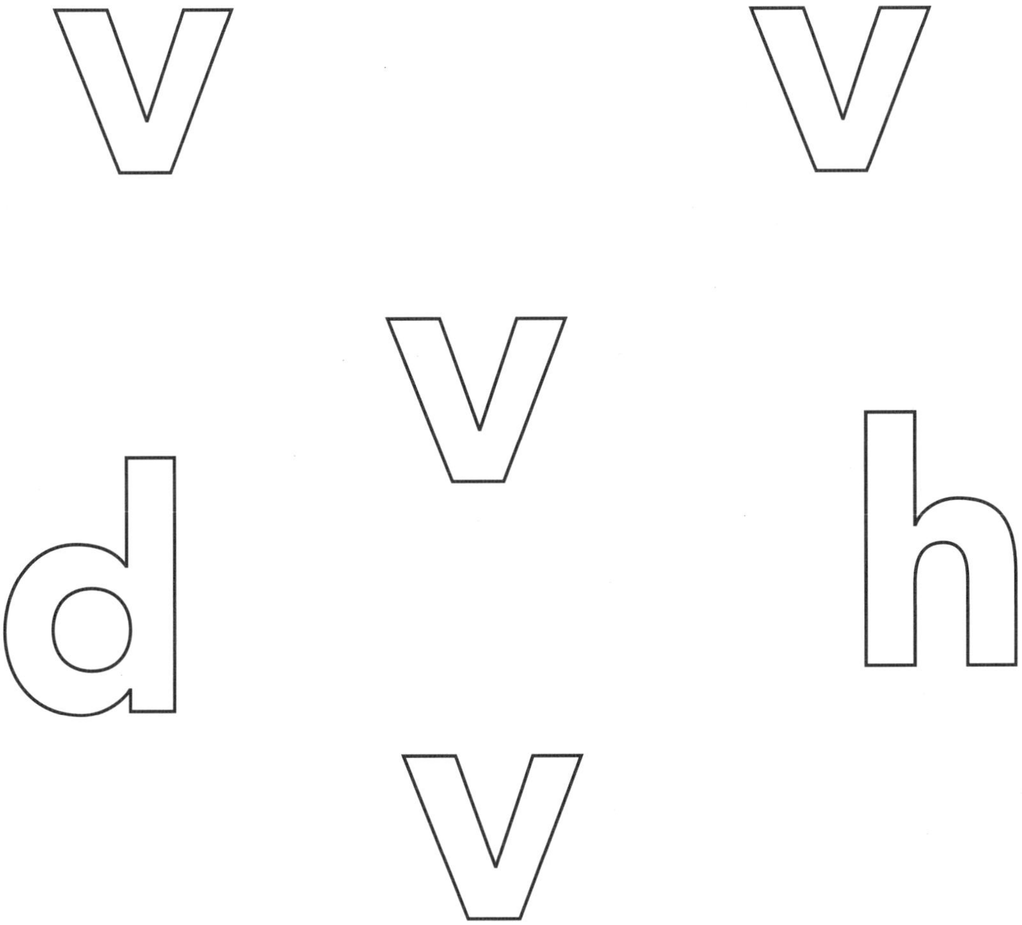

Primary Sound *v*

Name: ______________________ **Date:** ____________

Directions: Write the missing *v*'s. Color the pictures.

1.

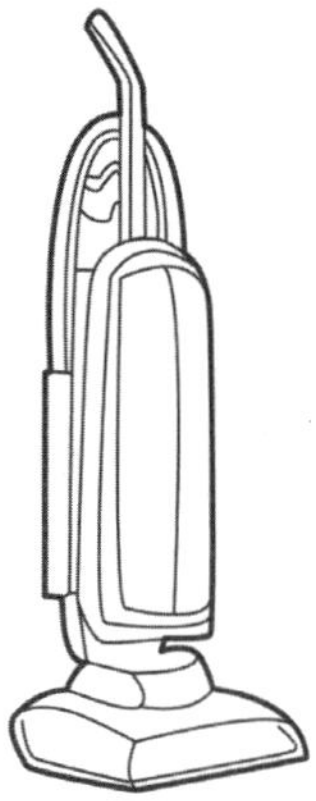

___acuum

2.

___an

3.

___est

4.

___ine

Name: ______________________________ **Date:** ________________

Directions: Trace and write.

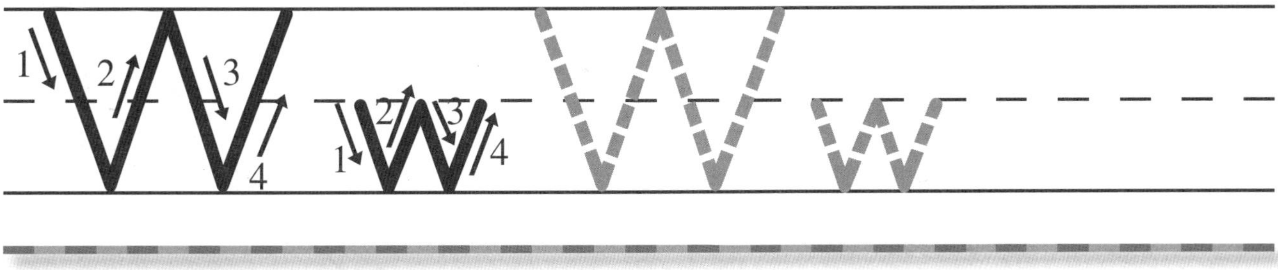

Directions: Color the *w*'s.

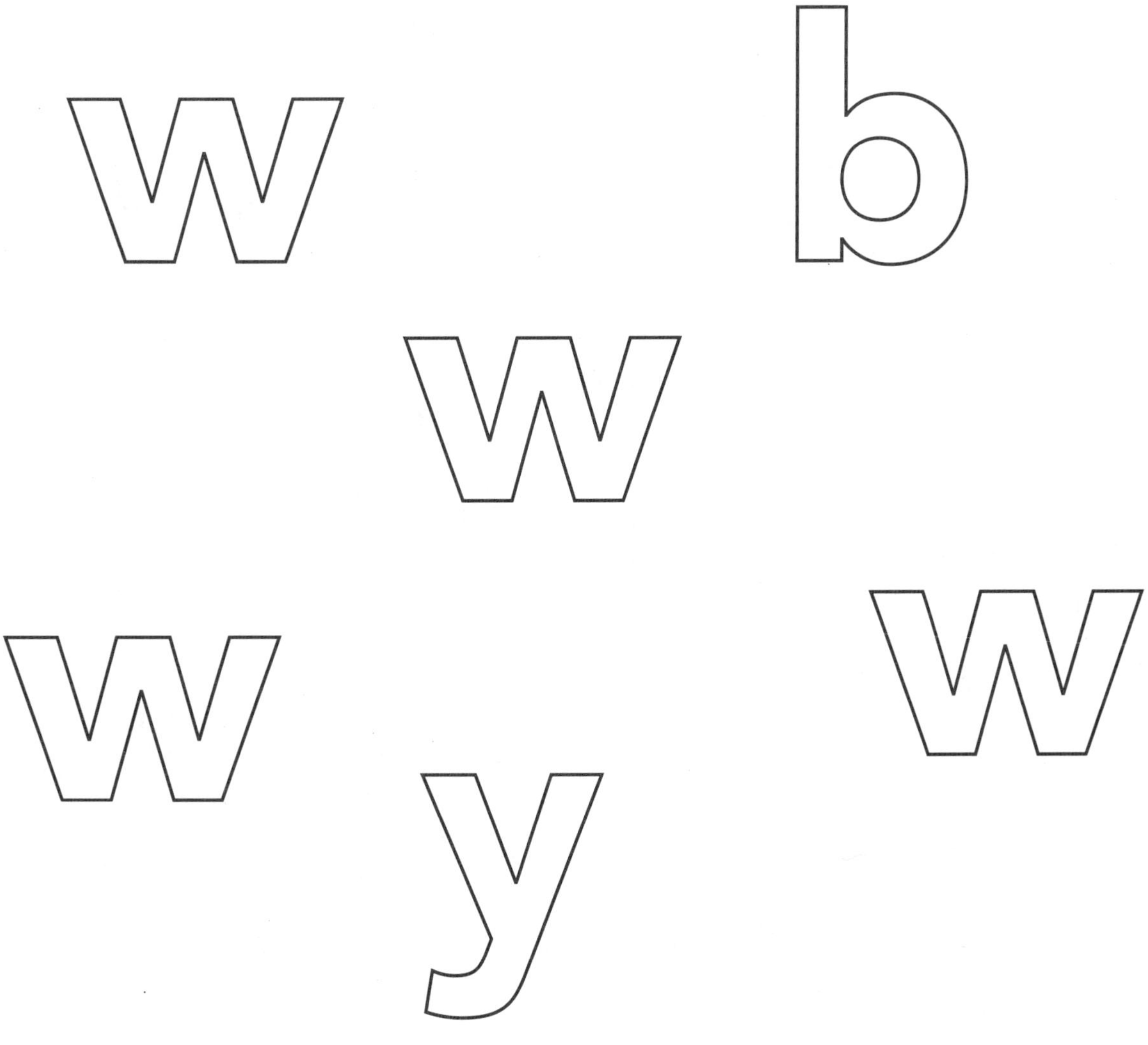

Primary Sound *w*

Name: ______________________ **Date:** ____________

Directions: Write the missing *w*'s. Color the pictures.

1.

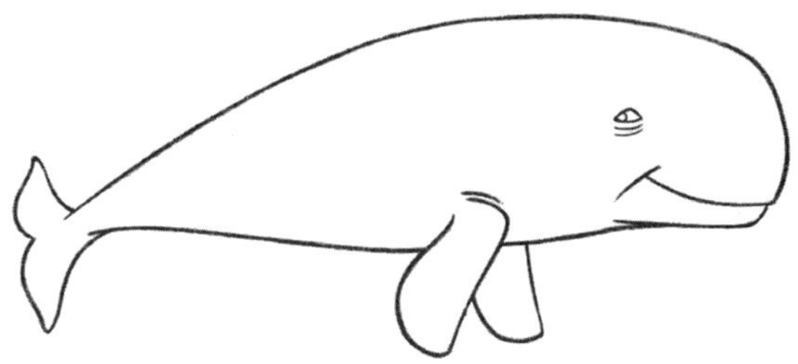

___hale

2.

___and

3.

___ig

4.

___olf

Name: ______________________________ **Date:** ________________

Directions: Trace and write.

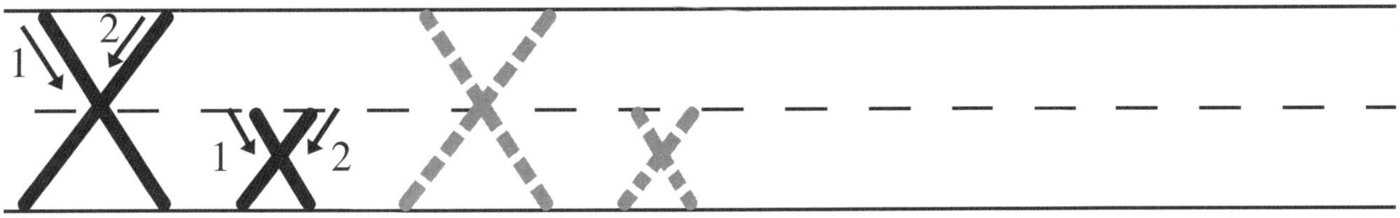

Directions: Color the *x*'s.

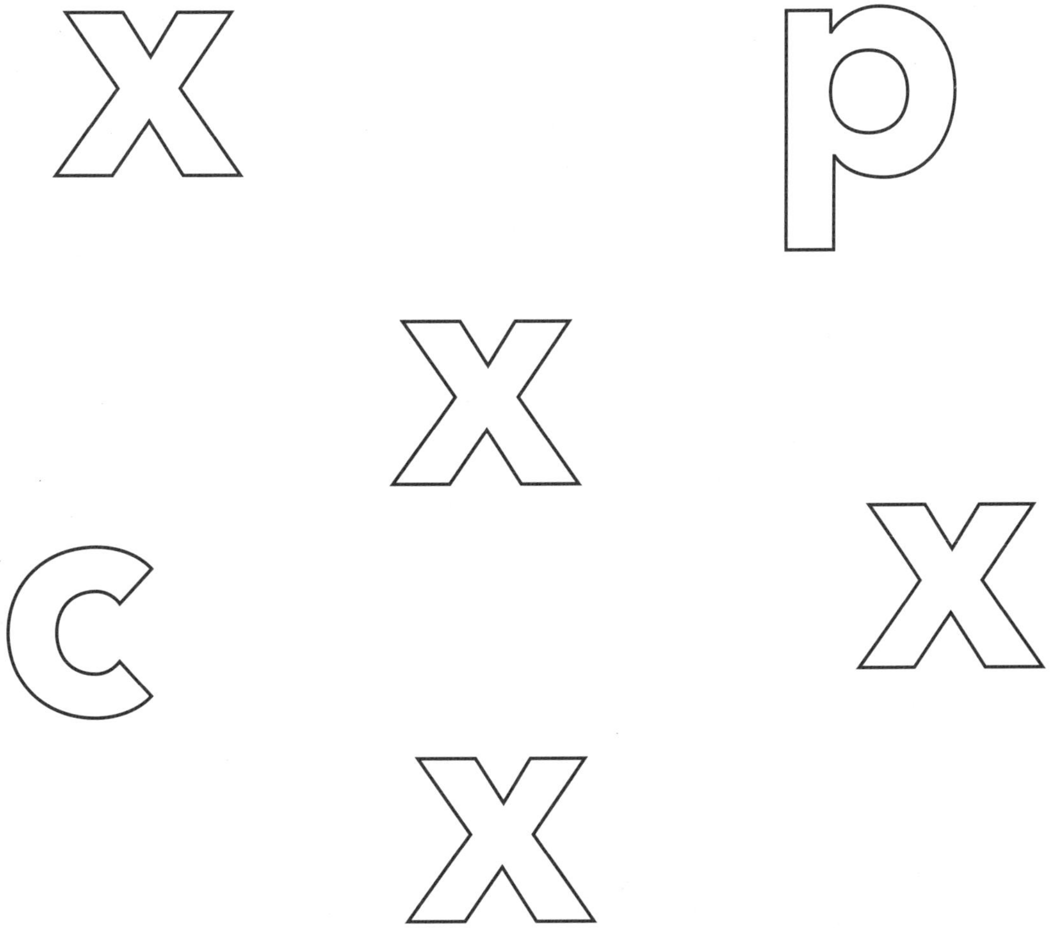

Primary Sound *x*

Name: ______________________________ **Date:** ____________

Directions: Write the missing *x*'s. Color the pictures.

1\.

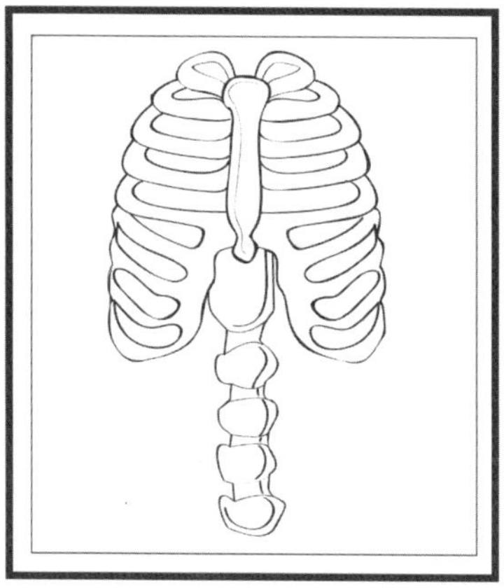

_ray

2\.

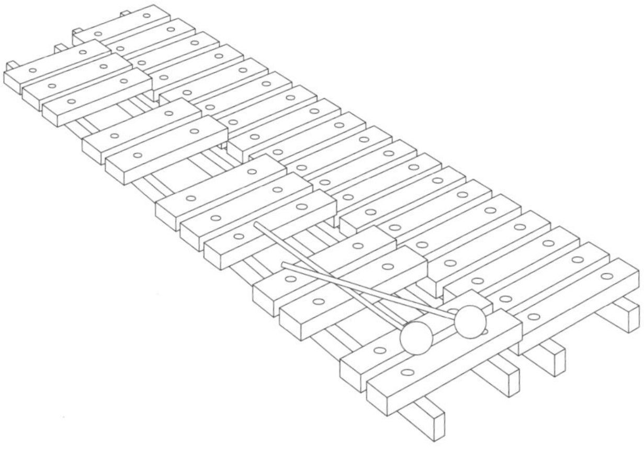

_ylophone

Primary Sound *y*

Name: ______________________ **Date:** ______________

Directions: Trace and write.

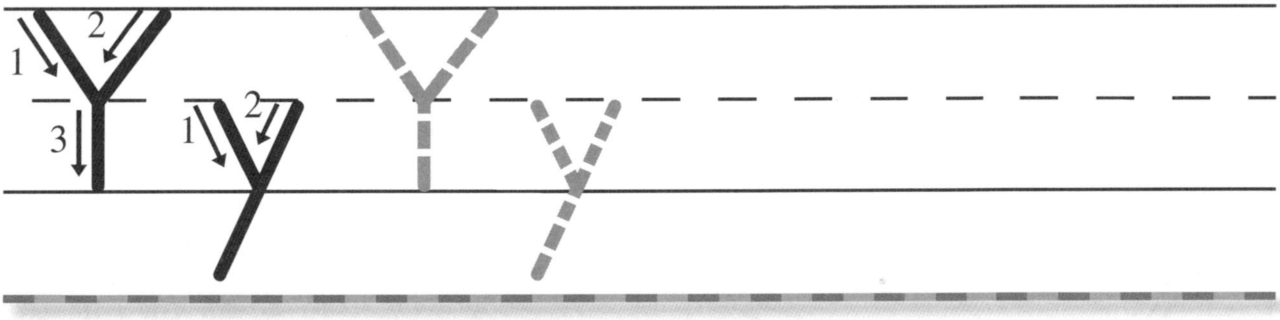

Directions: Color the *y*'s.

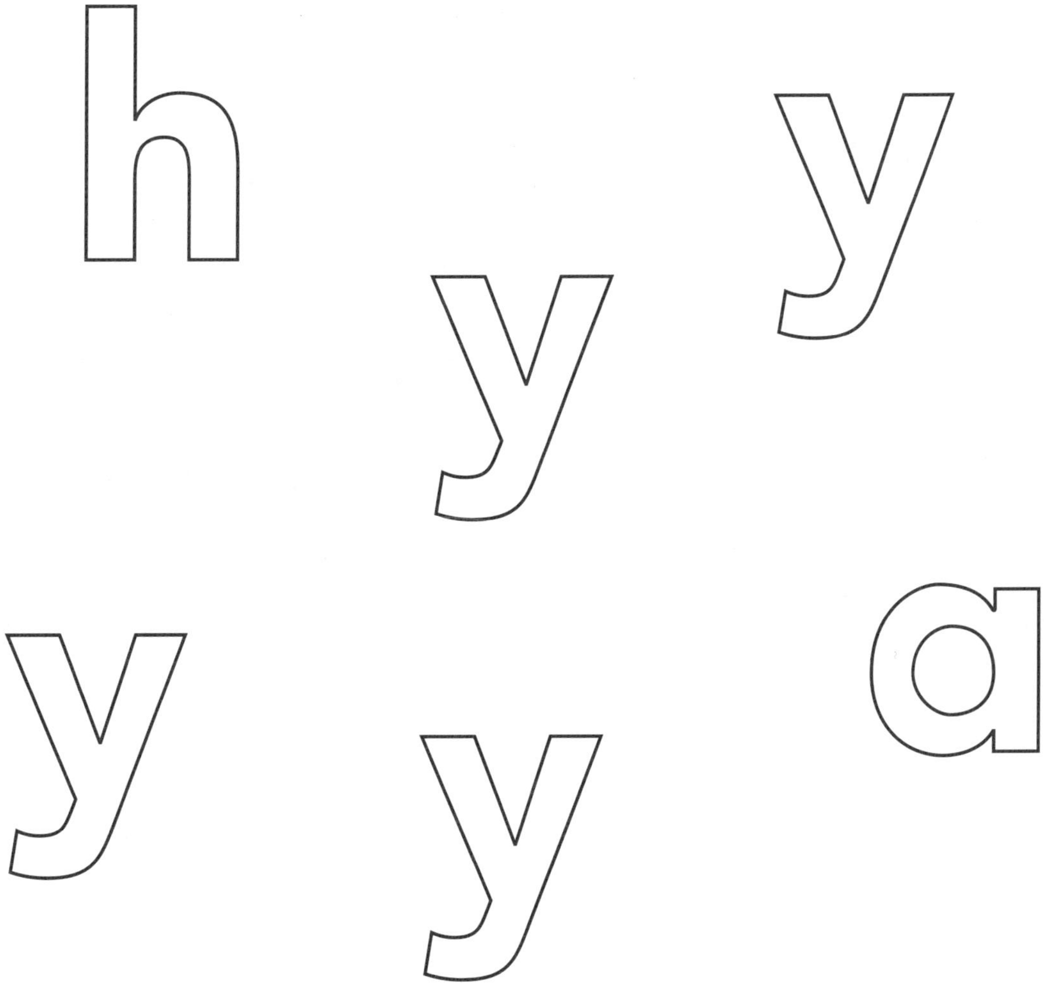

Primary Sound *y*

Name: ______________________________ **Date:** ______________

Directions: Write the missing *y*'s. Color the pictures.

1. 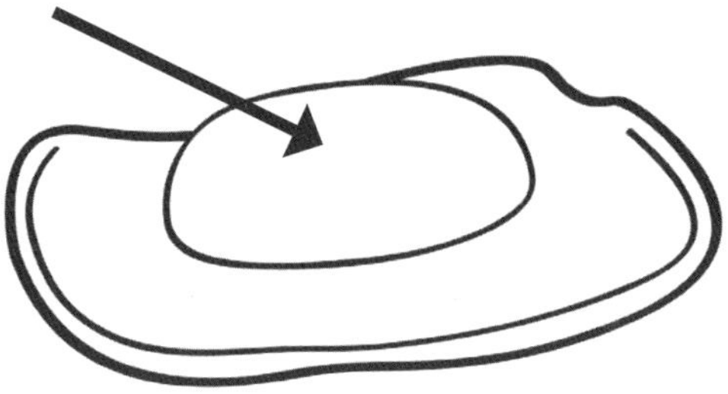 ___olk	2.  ___awn
3.  ___ak	4.  ___ogurt

Name: ______________________ **Date:** ______________

Directions: Trace and write.

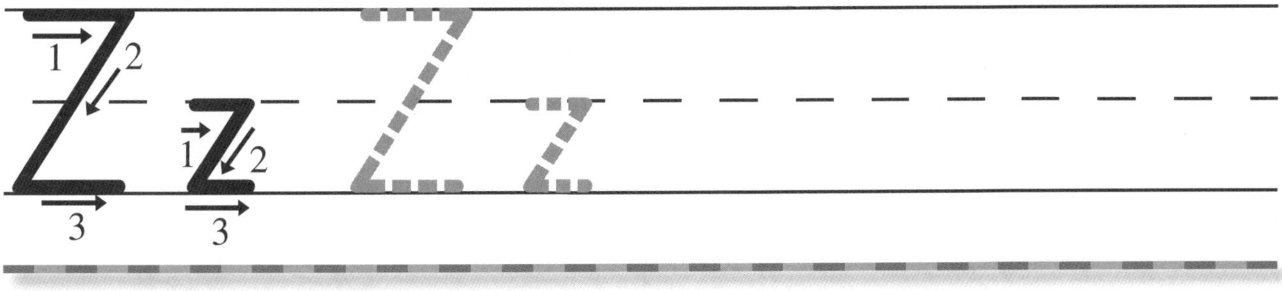

Directions: Color the *z*'s.

z u

z

f z

z

Primary Sound z

Name: ______________________________ **Date:** ______________

Directions: Write the missing *z*'s. Color the pictures.

1.

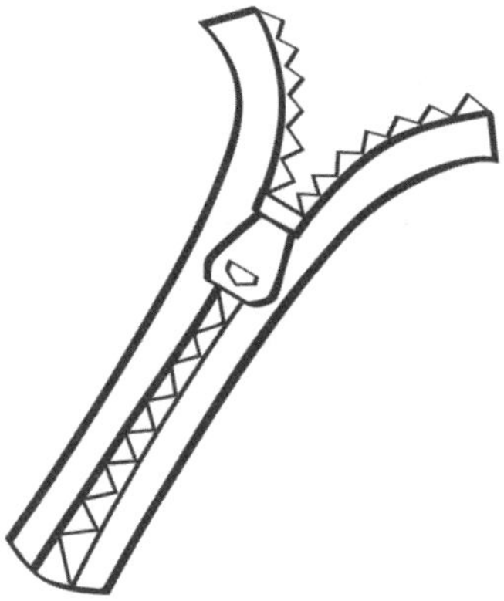

___ipper

2.

___ebra

3.

___ero

4.

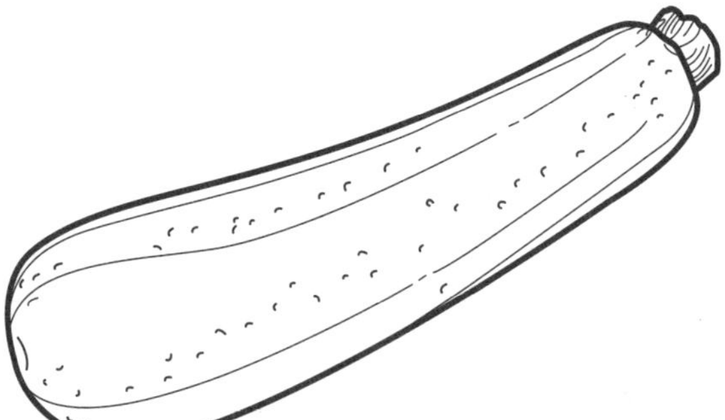

___ucchini

Name: ____________________ **Date:** ______________

Directions: Write the letter *a*. Draw a line from each word to its picture.

1. c a p

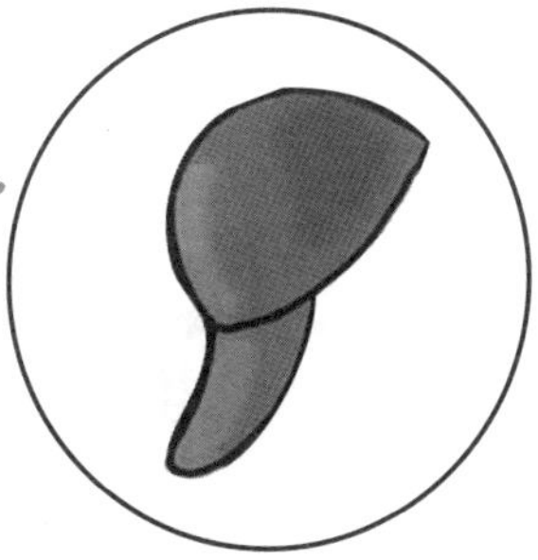

2. b ___ t

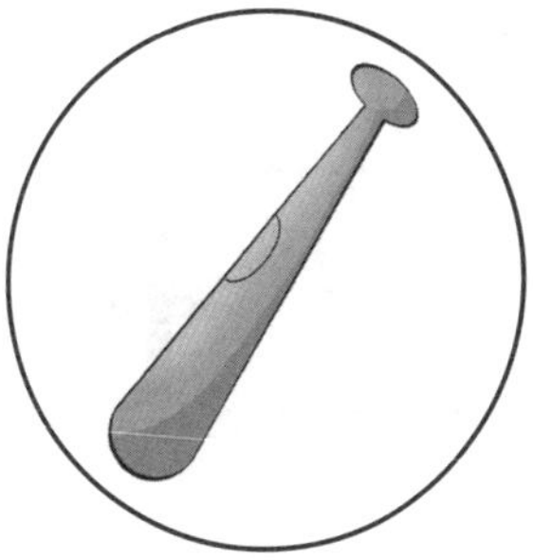

3. c ___ n

4. c ___ t

Short Vowel *a*

Name: ______________________ **Date:** ____________

Directions: Write the letter *a*. Draw a line from each word to its picture.

1. p __a__ n

2. h ____ m

3. r ____ t

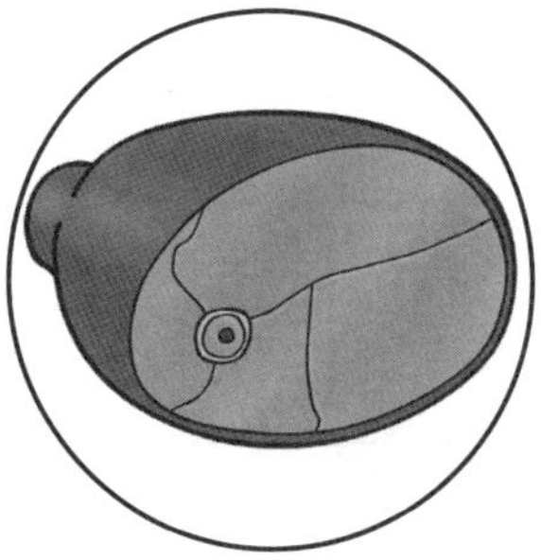

4. m ____ t

Name: ______________________ Date: ______________

Directions: Write the letter *e*. Draw a line from each word to its picture.

1. h e n

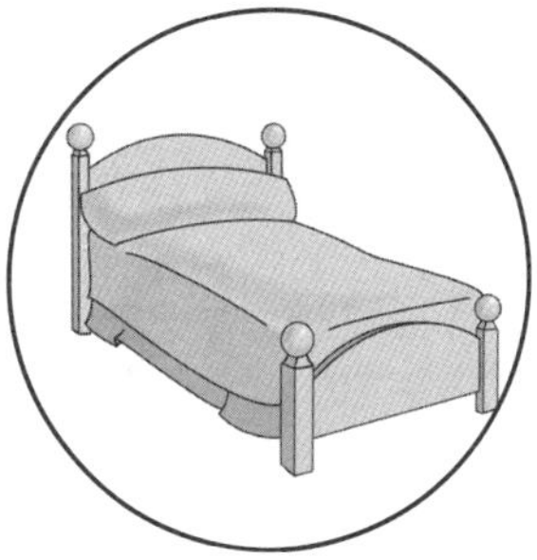

2. b ____ d

3. l ____ g

4. b ____ ll

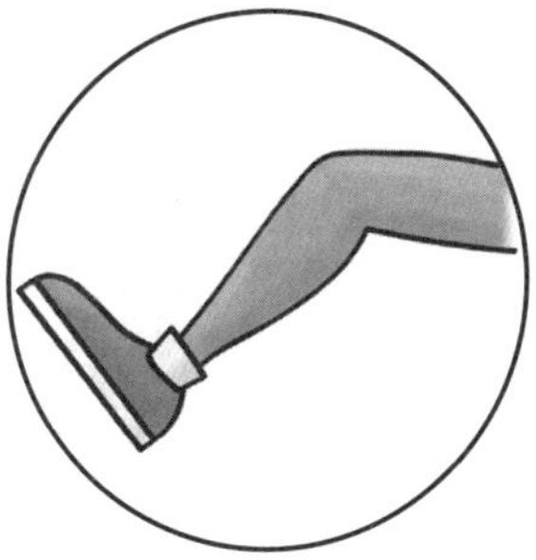

Short Vowel e

Name: ______________________ **Date:** ____________

Directions: Write the letter *e*. Draw a line from each word to its picture.

1. t ___ n

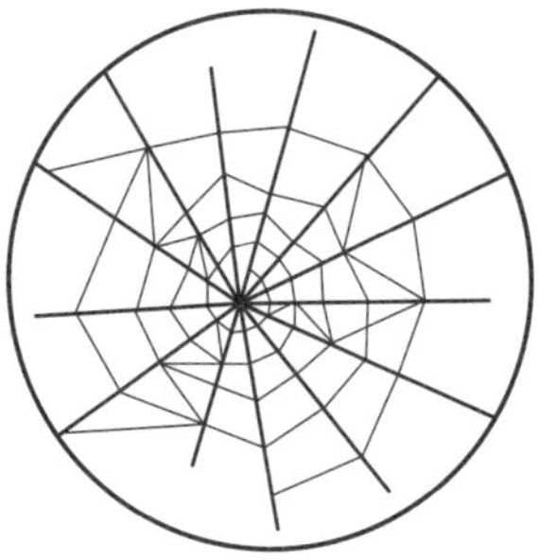

2. w ___ b

3. p ___ n

4. w ___ t

Name: ______________________ **Date:** ____________

Directions: Write the letter *i*. Draw a line from each word to its picture.

1. l _i_ p

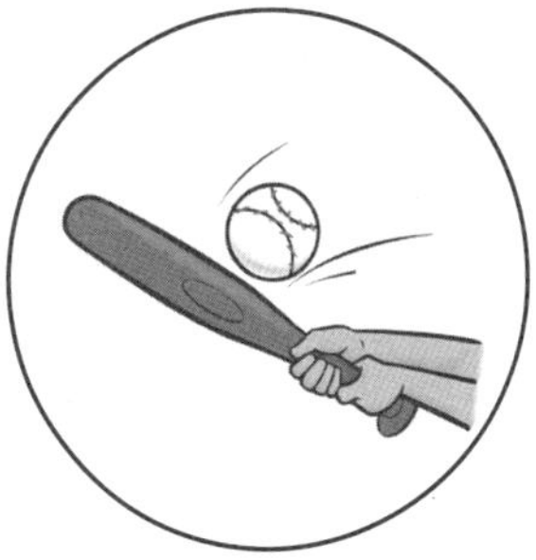

2. h ___ t

3. s ___ p

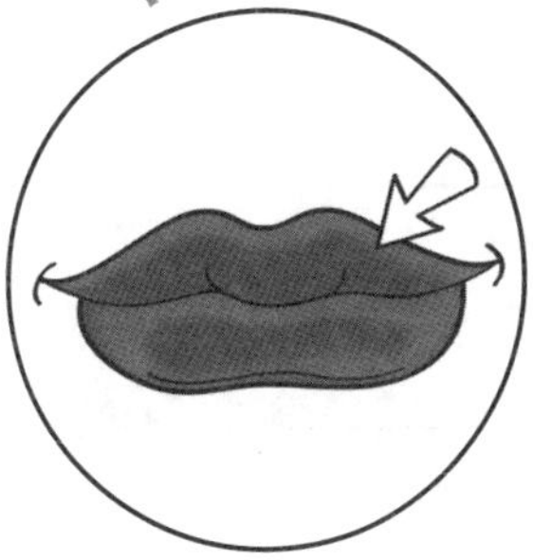

4. s ___ x

Short Vowel *i*

Name: ______________________ **Date:** __________

Directions: Write the letter *i*. Draw a line from each word to its picture.

1. d i g

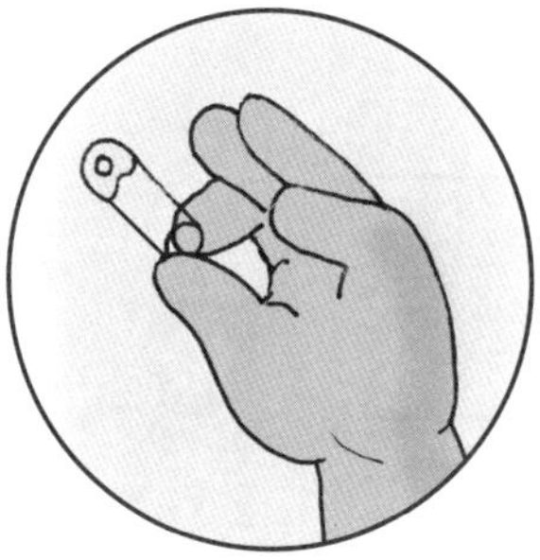

2. p __ n

3. f __ g

4. p __ g

Name: ______________________ **Date:** ______________

Directions: Write the letter *o*. Draw a line from each word to its picture.

1. l __ g

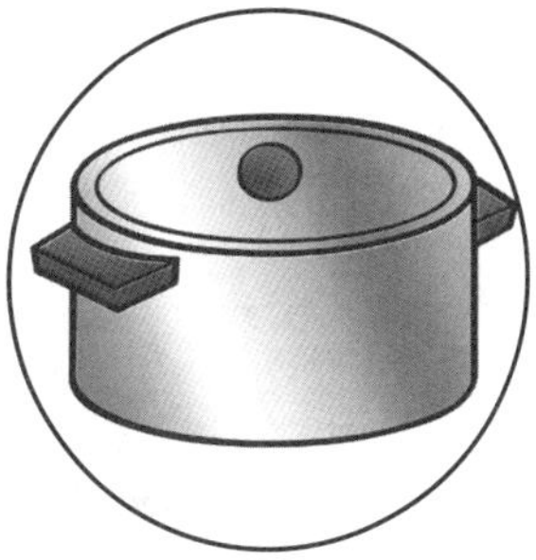

2. p __ t

3. m __ p

4. d __ ll

Short Vowel *o*

Name: ______________________ **Date:** ____________

Directions: Write the letter *o*. Draw a line from each word to its picture.

1. d ___ g

2. c ___ t

3. t ___ p

4. l ___ ck

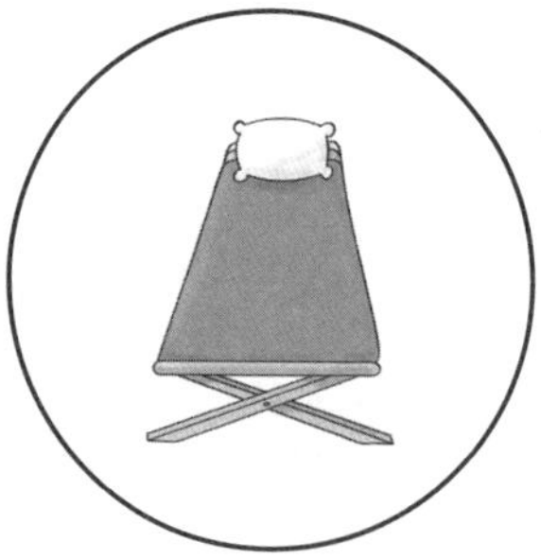

Name: ______________________ **Date:** ______________

Directions: Write the letter *u*. Draw a line from each word to its picture.

1. j u g

2. d ___ g

3. b ___ g

4. c ___ p

Short Vowel *u*

Name: ______________________________ **Date:** ____________

Directions: Write the letter *u*. Draw a line from each word to its picture.

1. s u n
2. p ___ p
3. n ___ t
4. b ___ s

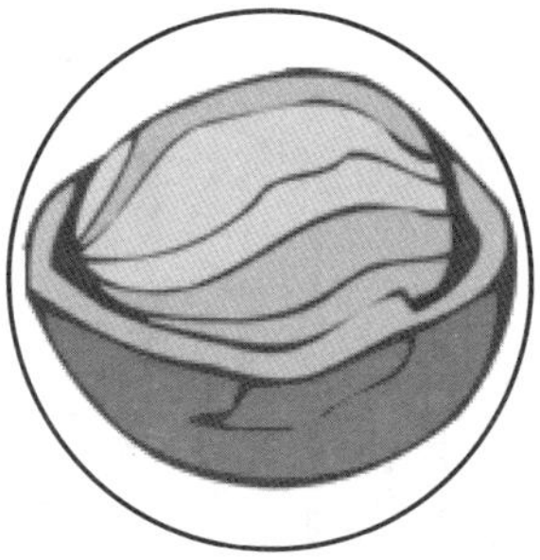

Name: ______________________ **Date:** ______________

Directions: Write the letters *ai*. Draw a line from each word to its picture.

1. m ai l

2. p ____ l

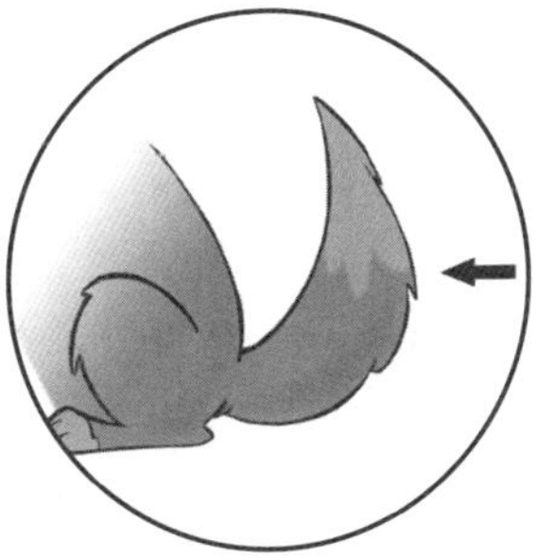

3. n ____ l

4. t ____ l

Long Vowel *a*

Name: ______________________ **Date:** ____________

Directions: Write the letters *a* and *e*. Draw a line from each word to its picture.

1. r a k e
2. c ___ k ___
3. t ___ p ___
4. g ___ t ___

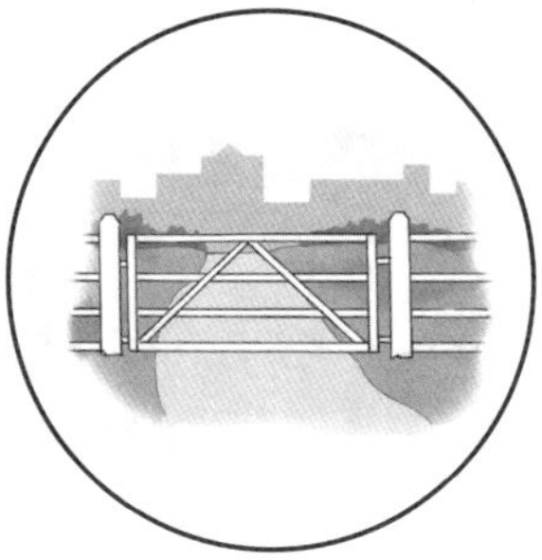

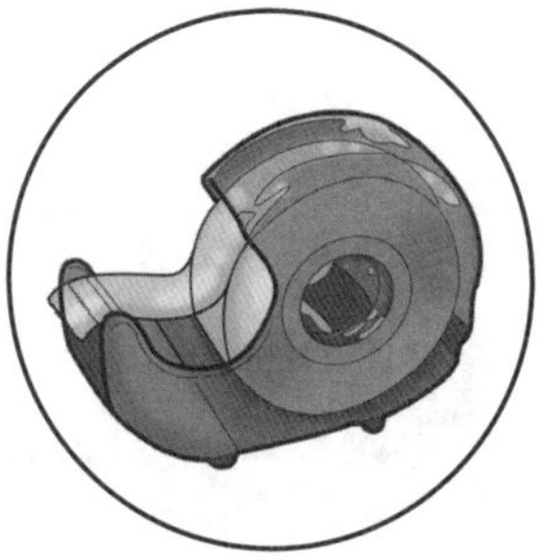

Long Vowel e

Name: ______________________ **Date:** ____________

Directions: Write the letters *ee*. Draw a line from each word to its picture.

1. wh ee l

2. sh ____ p

3. qu ____ n

4. b ____

Long Vowel e

Name: ______________________________ **Date:** _____________

Directions: Write the letters *ea*. Draw a line from each word to its picture.

1. m ea t

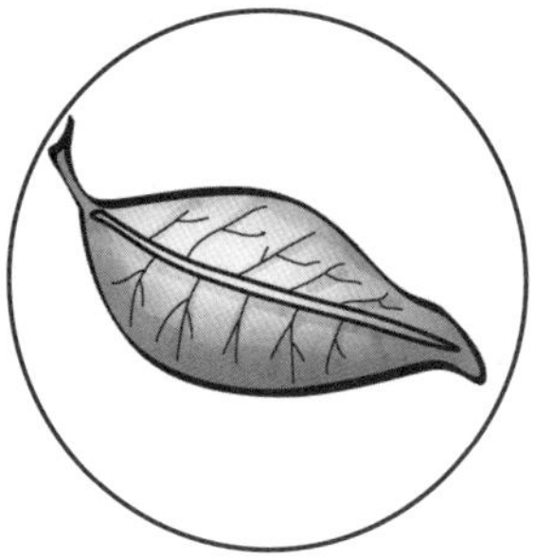

2. p ______ s

3. l ______ f

4. s ______ l

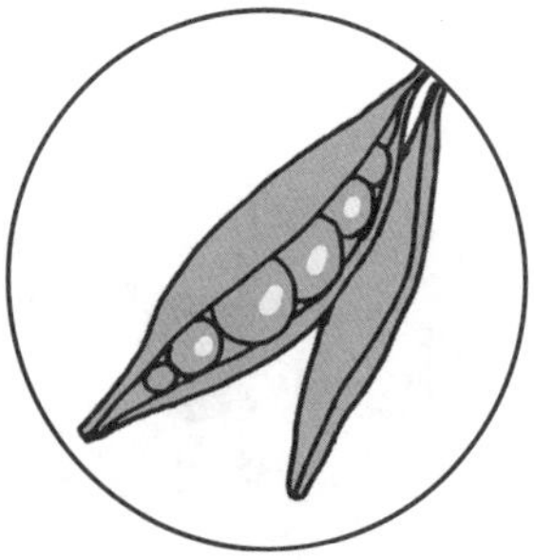

Long Vowel *i*

Name: ____________________ **Date:** ______________

Directions: Write the letters *i* and *e*. Draw a line from each word to its picture.

1. d i c e

2. f ___ r ___

3. f ___ v ___

4. k ___ t ___

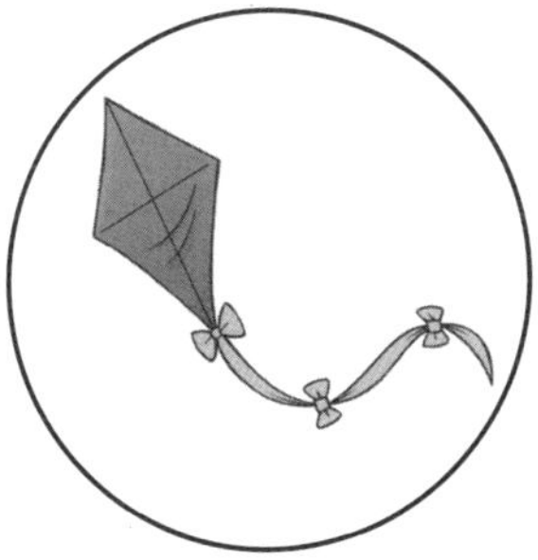

Long Vowel *i*

Name: ______________________ **Date:** ____________

Directions: Write the letter *i*. Draw a line from each word to its picture.

1. i ce

2. ___ sland

3. ___ dea

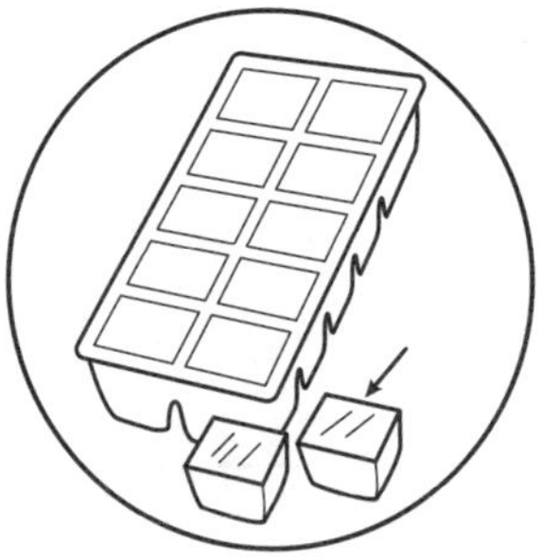

4. ___ ron

Name: ______________________ **Date:** ______________

Directions: Write the letters *oa*. Draw a line from each word to its picture.

1. b oa t 

2. g ___ t 

3. t ___ d 

4. c ___ t 

Long Vowel *o*

Name: ______________________ **Date:** ____________

Directions: Write the letters *o* and *e* in each word. Read the words. Draw a line from each word to its picture.

1. r o s e

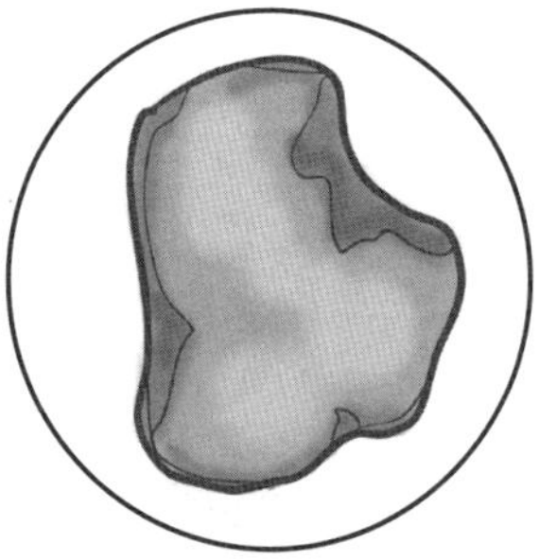

2. b ___ n ___

3. c ___ n ___

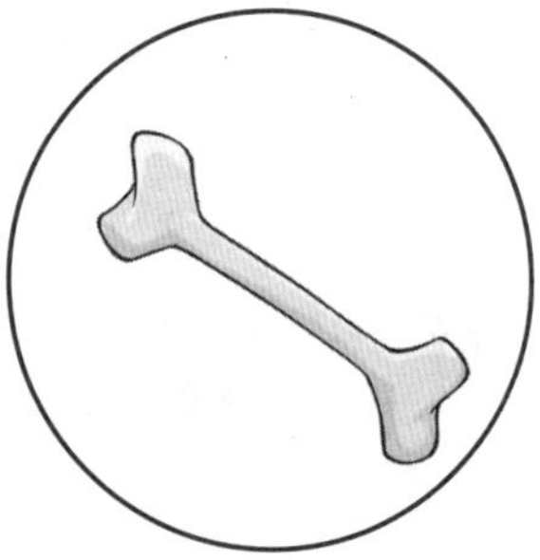

4. st ___ n ___

Name: ______________________ **Date:** ______________

Directions: Write the letters *u* and *e* in each word. Read the words. Draw a line from each word to its picture.

1. m u l e

2. c __ b __

3. t __ b __

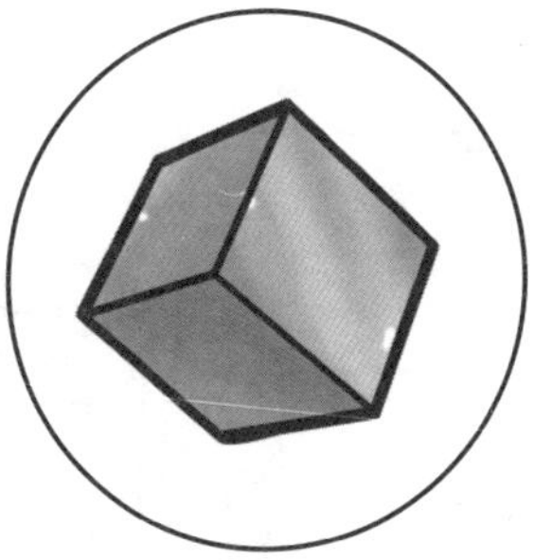

4. t __ n __

Long Vowel *u*

Name: ______________________ **Date:** ____________

Directions: Write the letter *u* in each word. Read the words. Draw a line from each word to its picture.

1. u nicycle

2. ______ niform

3. ______ tensils

4. ______ nicorn

Additional Practice

Name: ______________________________ **Date:** ________________

Directions: Trace the letters.

 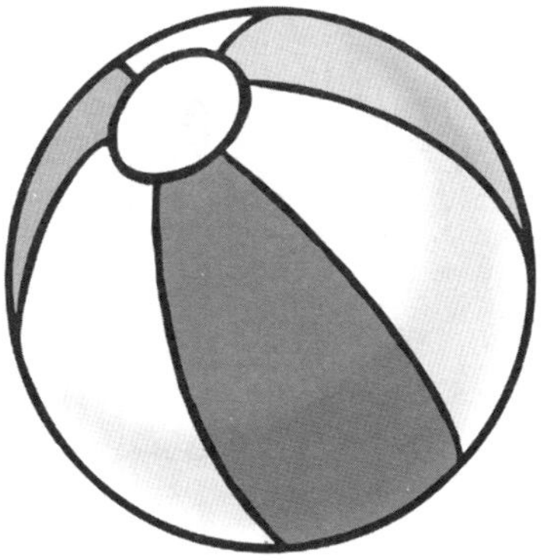 

Aa Bb Cc

 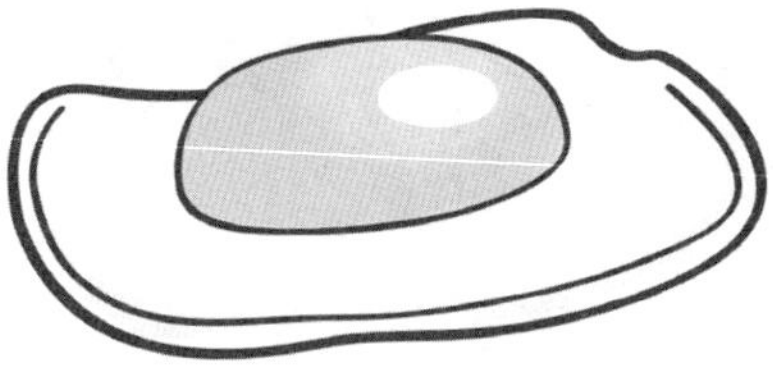 

Dd Ee Ff

Additional Practice

Name: ______________________________ **Date:** _____________

Directions: Trace the letters.

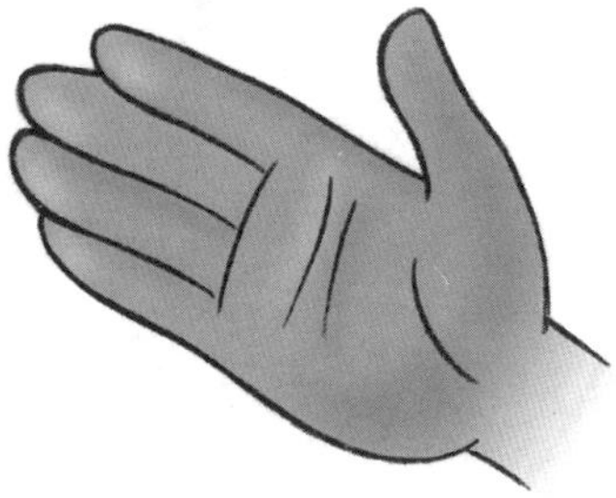

Gg Hh Ii

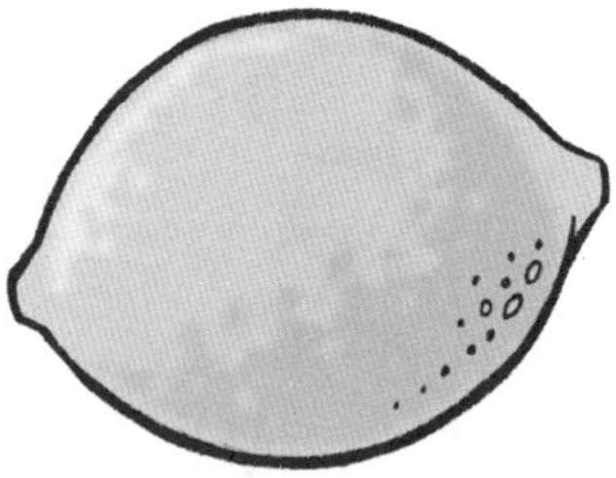

Jj Kk Ll

Additional Practice

Name: ______________________ **Date:** ______________

Directions: Trace the letters.

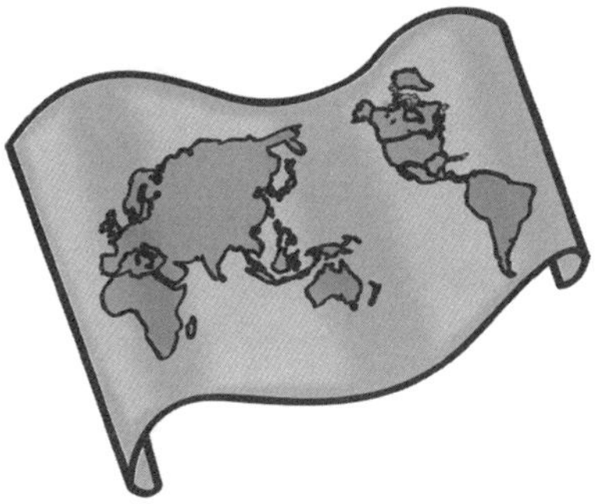
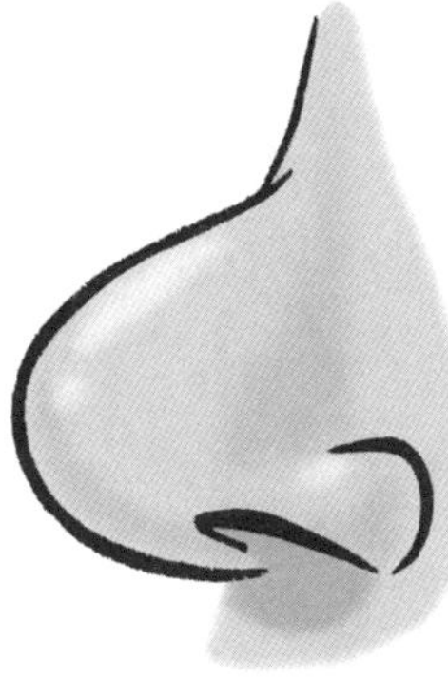

Mm Nn Oo

Pp Qq Rr

Additional Practice

Name: ______________________ Date: __________

Directions: Trace the letters.

Ss Tt Uu

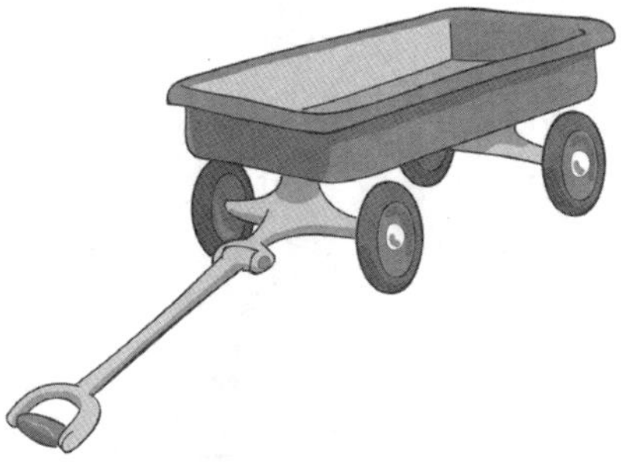
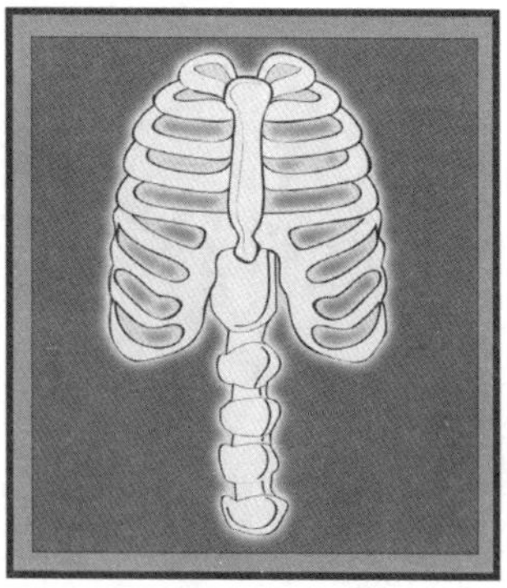

Vv Ww Xx

Name: ______________________ **Date:** ______________

Directions: Trace the letters.

Yy Zz

References Cited

Chall, Jeanne S. 1995. *Learning to read: The great debate*, 3rd ed. Orlando: Harcourt Brace.

Cook, Vivian. 2004. *Accomodating brocolli in the cemetary: Or, why can't anybody spell?* New York: Touchstone.

Fry, Edward B., and Jacqueline E. Kress. 2006. *The reading teacher's book of lists*, 5th ed. San Francisco: Jossey-Bass.

Griffith, Priscilla L., and Mary W. Olson. 1992. Phonemic awareness helps beginning readers break the code. *The Reading Teacher*, 45: 516–523.

Juel, C. 1988. Learning to read and write: A longitudinal study of 54 children from first to fourth grades. *Journal of Educational Psychology*, 78: 243–255.

Lomax, Richels G., and Lomax M. McGee. 1987. Young children's concepts about print and meaning: Toward a model of reading acquisition. *Reading Research Quarterly*, 22: 237–256.

National Governors Association Center for Best Practices and Council of Chief State School Officers. 2010. Common core standards. http://corestandards.org/the-standards.

National Reading Panel. 2000. *Report of the National Reading Panel: Teaching children to read*. Washington, DC: Donald N. Langenberg, chair.

Tunmer, William E., and Richard A. Nesdale. 1985. Phonemic segmentation skill and beginning reading. *Journal of Educational Psychology*, 77: 417–427.

Answer Key

page 11

Primary Sound *a*

Name: Date:

Directions: Trace and write.

Aa Aa Aa

Directions: Color the a's.

a a b c a a

page 15

Primary Sound *c*

Name: Date:

Directions: Trace and write.

Cc Cc Cc

Directions: Color the c's.

c h b c c c

page 19

Primary Sound *e*

Name: Date:

Directions: Trace and write.

Ee Ee Ee

Directions: Color the e's.

c e e e e l

page 12

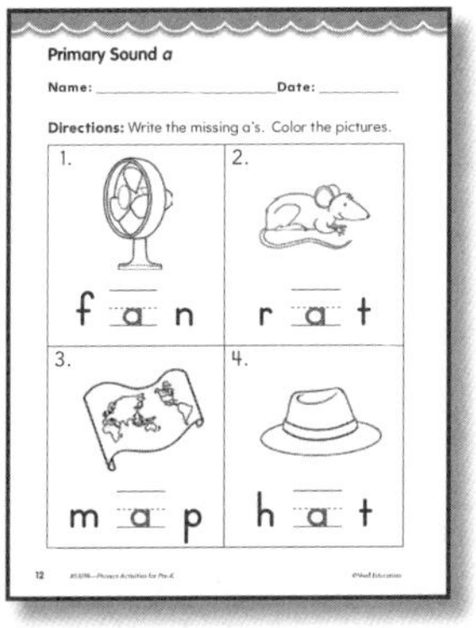

Primary Sound *a*

Name: Date:

Directions: Write the missing a's. Color the pictures.

1. f a n
2. r a t
3. m a p
4. h a t

page 16

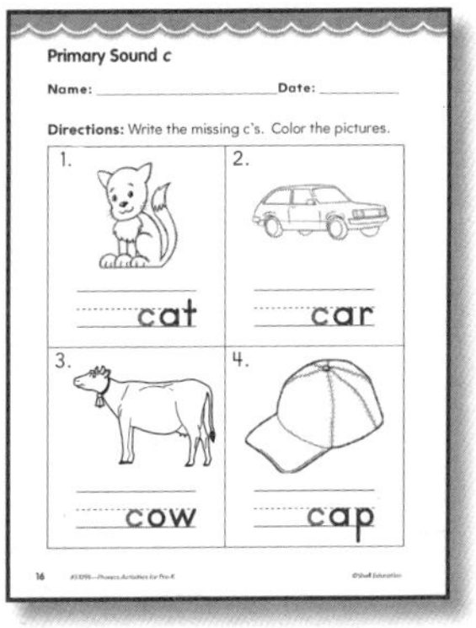

Primary Sound *c*

Name: Date:

Directions: Write the missing c's. Color the pictures.

1. cat
2. car
3. cow
4. cap

page 20

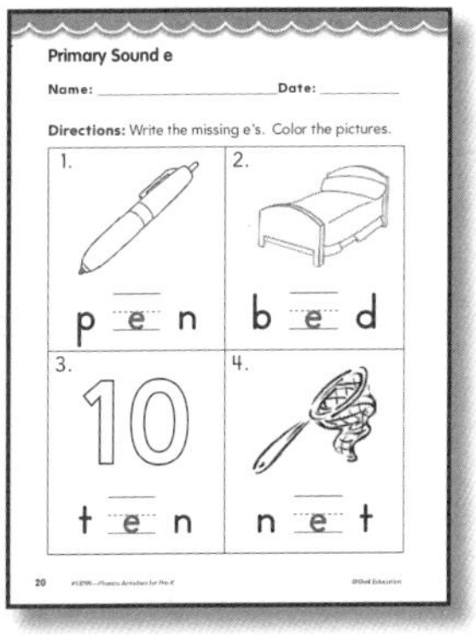

Primary Sound e

Name: Date:

Directions: Write the missing e's. Color the pictures.

1. p e n
2. b e d
3. t e n
4. n e t

page 13

Primary Sound *b*

Name: Date:

Directions: Trace and write.

Bb Bb Bb

Directions: Color the b's.

c b b b b f

page 17

Primary Sound *d*

Name: Date:

Directions: Trace and write.

Dd Dd Dd

Directions: Color the d's.

d d d b d a

page 21

Primary Sound *f*

Name: Date:

Directions: Trace and write.

Ff Ff Ff

Directions: Color the f's.

f g f e f f

page 14

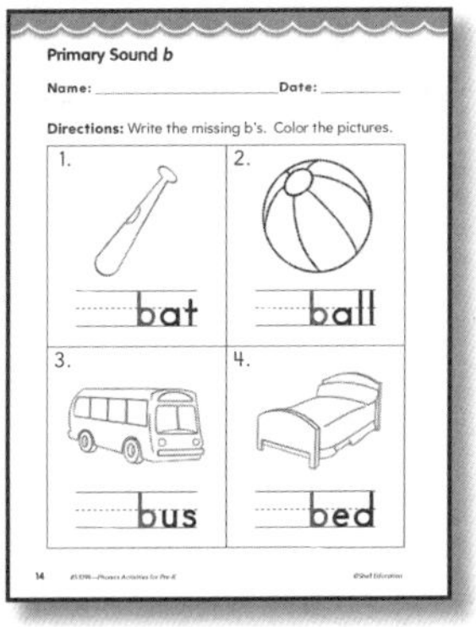

Primary Sound *b*

Name: Date:

Directions: Write the missing b's. Color the pictures.

1. bat
2. ball
3. bus
4. bed

page 18

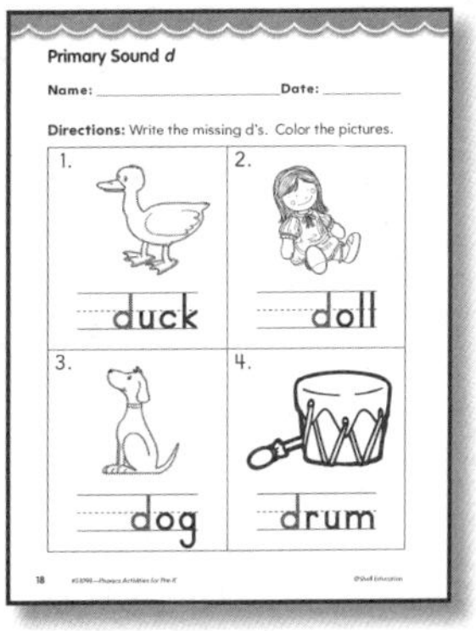

Primary Sound *d*

Name: Date:

Directions: Write the missing d's. Color the pictures.

1. duck
2. doll
3. dog
4. drum

page 22

Primary Sound *f*

Name: Date:

Directions: Write the missing f's. Color the pictures.

1. fork
2. fan
3. fox
4. frog

page 23

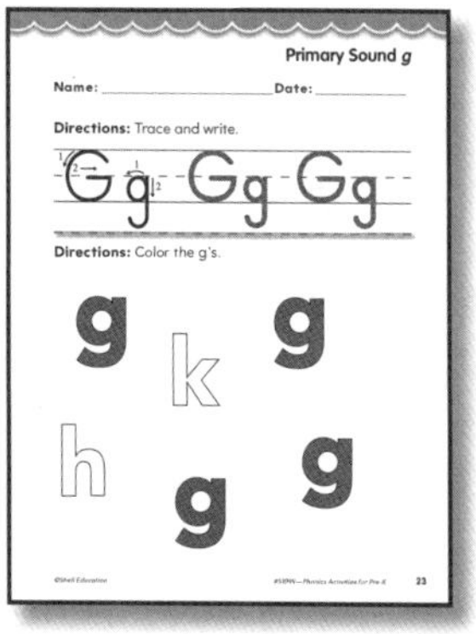
Primary Sound *g*

Name: ____________ Date: ________

Directions: Trace and write.

Gg Gg Gg

Directions: Color the g's.

g k g h g g

page 24

Primary Sound *g*

Name: ____________ Date: ________

Directions: Write the missing g's. Color the pictures.

1. gift
2. gate
3. girl
4. goat

page 25

Primary Sound *h*

Name: ____________ Date: ________

Directions: Trace and write.

Hh Hh Hh

Directions: Color the h's.

c h h h h l

page 26

Primary Sound *h*

Name: ____________ Date: ________

Directions: Write the missing h's. Color the pictures.

1. hand
2. ham
3. hat
4. hen

page 27

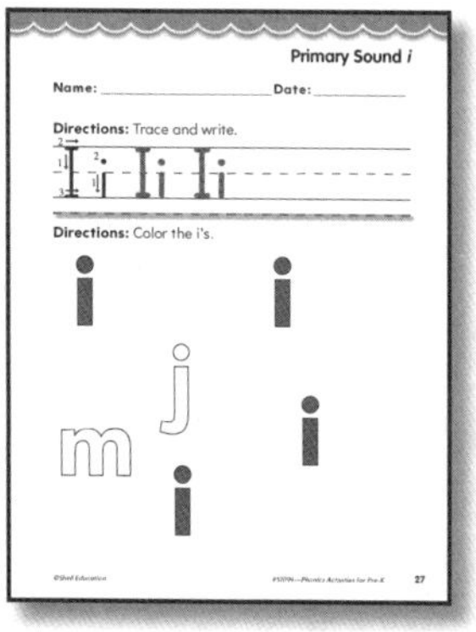
Primary Sound *i*

Name: ____________ Date: ________

Directions: Trace and write.

Ii Ii Ii

Directions: Color the i's.

i i j m i i

page 28

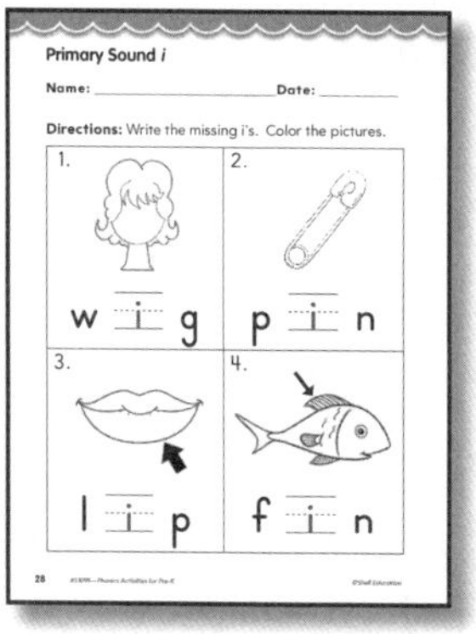
Primary Sound *i*

Name: ____________ Date: ________

Directions: Write the missing i's. Color the pictures.

1. w i g
2. p i n
3. l i p
4. f i n

page 29

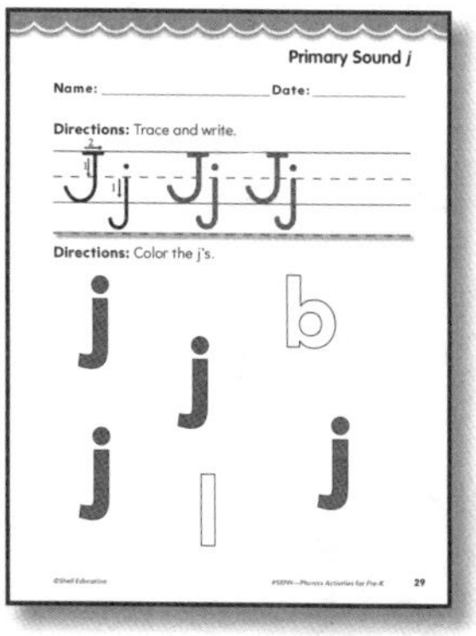
Primary Sound *j*

Name: ____________ Date: ________

Directions: Trace and write.

Jj Jj Jj

Directions: Color the j's.

j b j j l j

page 30

Primary Sound *j*

Name: ____________ Date: ________

Directions: Write the missing j's. Color the pictures.

1. jet
2. jar
3. jug
4. jam

page 31

Primary Sound *k*

Name: ____________ Date: ________

Directions: Trace and write.

Kk Kk Kk

Directions: Color the k's.

k d k f k k

page 32

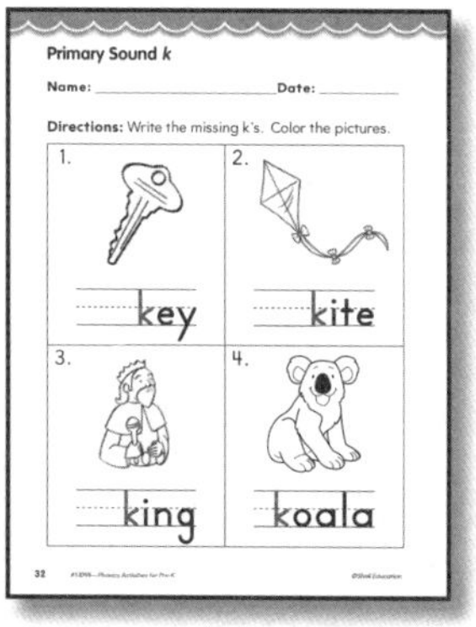
Primary Sound *k*

Name: ____________ Date: ________

Directions: Write the missing k's. Color the pictures.

1. key
2. kite
3. king
4. koala

page 33

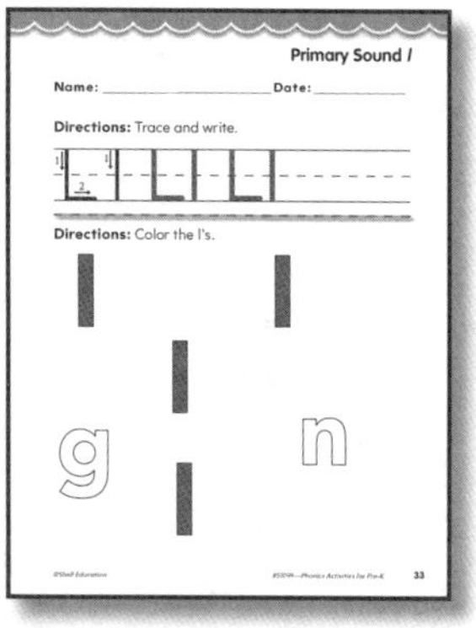
Primary Sound *l*

Name: ____________ Date: ________

Directions: Trace and write.

Ll Ll Ll

Directions: Color the l's.

l l l g n l

page 34

Primary Sound *l*

Name: ____________ Date: ________

Directions: Write the missing l's. Color the pictures.

1. lamp
2. lion
3. lock
4. log

page 35

Primary Sound m
Name: Date:
Directions: Trace and write.
Mm Mm Mm
Directions: Color the m's.
m n m m m p

page 39

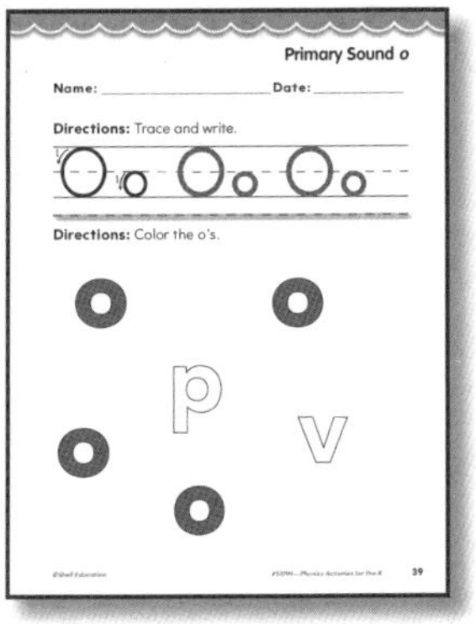
Primary Sound o
Name: Date:
Directions: Trace and write.
Oo Oo Oo
Directions: Color the o's.
o o p o v o

page 43

Primary Sound q
Name: Date:
Directions: Trace and write.
Qq Qq Qq
Directions: Color the q's.
q g q v q q

page 36

Primary Sound m
Name: Date:
Directions: Write the missing m's. Color the pictures.
1. moon 2. map 3. mop 4. mug

page 40

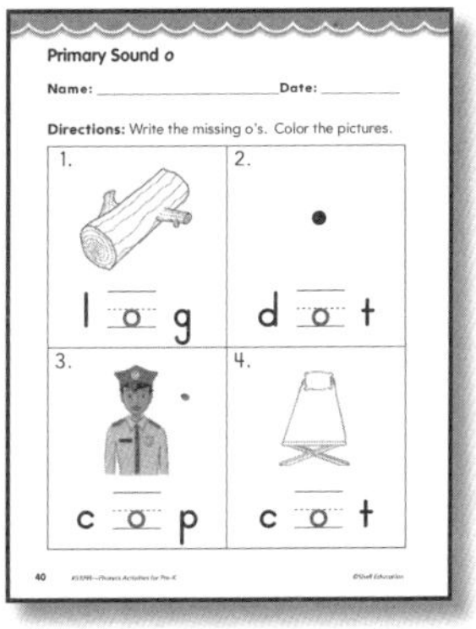
Primary Sound o
Name: Date:
Directions: Write the missing o's. Color the pictures.
1. l o g 2. d o t 3. c o p 4. c o t

page 44

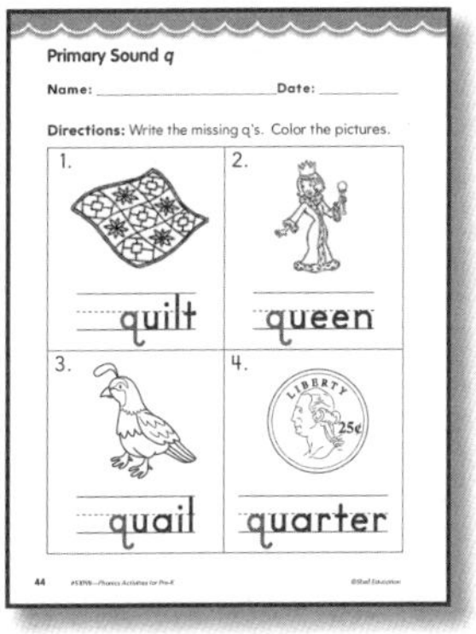
Primary Sound q
Name: Date:
Directions: Write the missing q's. Color the pictures.
1. quilt 2. queen 3. quail 4. quarter

page 37

Primary Sound n
Name: Date:
Directions: Trace and write.
Nn Nn Nn
Directions: Color the n's.
s n s n n n

page 41

Primary Sound p
Name: Date:
Directions: Trace and write.
Pp Pp Pp
Directions: Color the p's.
f p p p c p

page 45

Primary Sound r
Name: Date:
Directions: Trace and write.
Rr Rr Rr
Directions: Color the r's.
r r r m a r

page 38

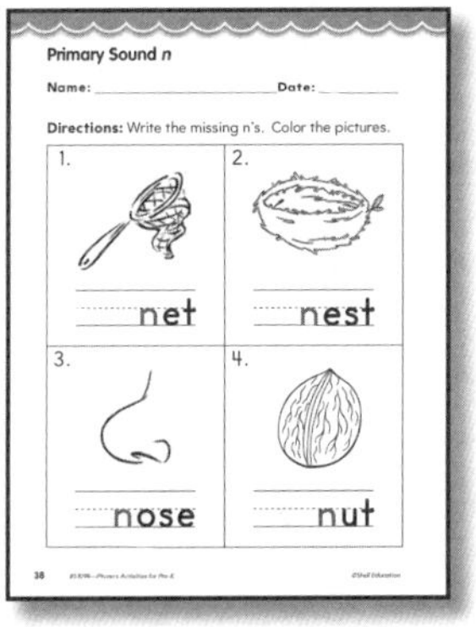
Primary Sound n
Name: Date:
Directions: Write the missing n's. Color the pictures.
1. net 2. nest 3. nose 4. nut

page 42

Primary Sound p
Name: Date:
Directions: Write the missing p's. Color the pictures.
1. panda 2. pan 3. pen 4. pig

page 46

Primary Sound r
Name: Date:
Directions: Write the missing r's. Color the pictures.
1. rest 2. rat 3. ring 4. rabbit

Answer Key *(cont.)*

page 47

page 48

page 49

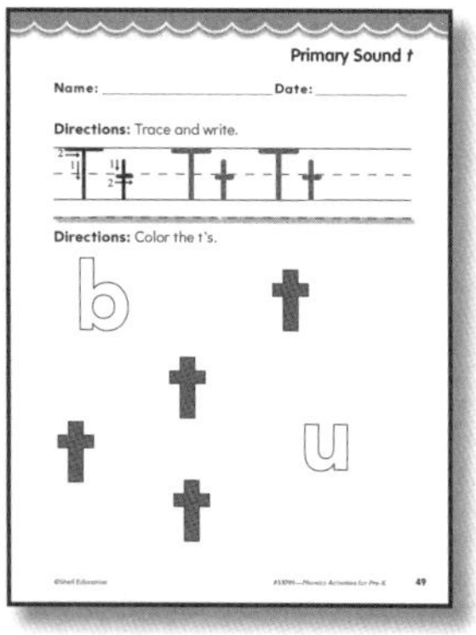

page 50

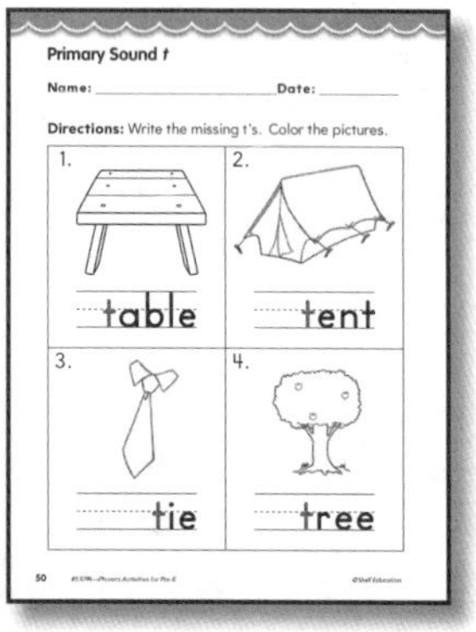

page 51

page 52

page 53

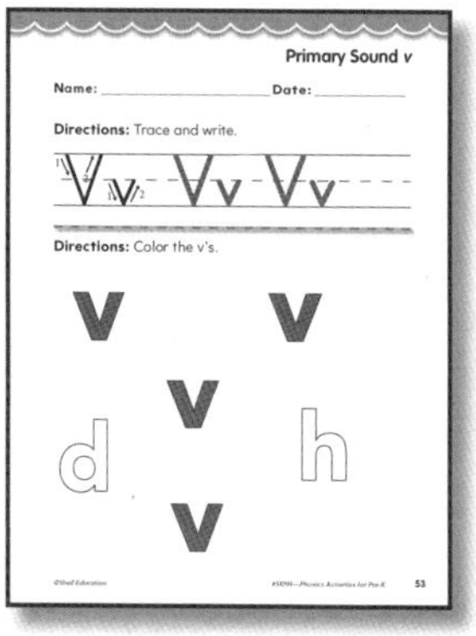

page 54

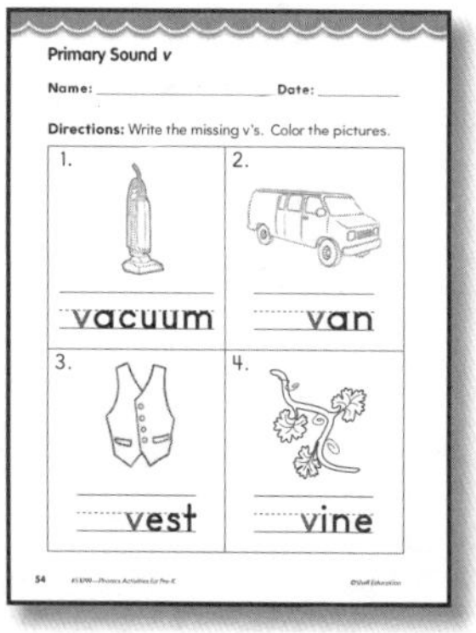

page 55

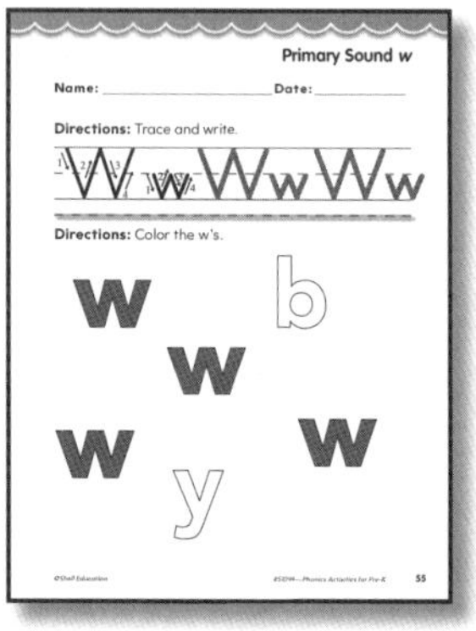

page 56

page 57

page 58

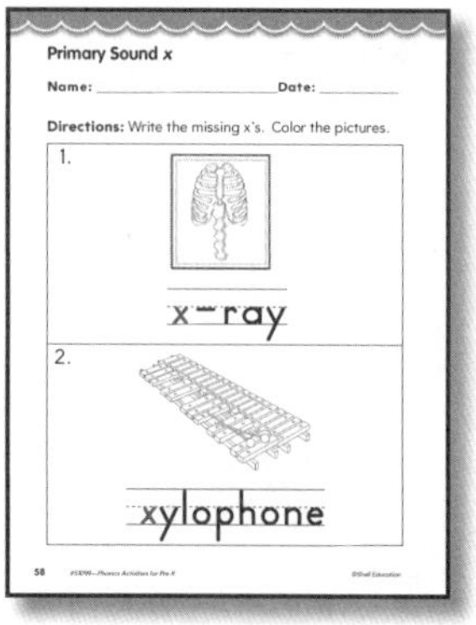

page 59

Primary Sound *y*

Name: ______________ Date: ________

Directions: Trace and write.

Yy Yy Yy

Directions: Color all of the y's.

h y y y y a

page 63

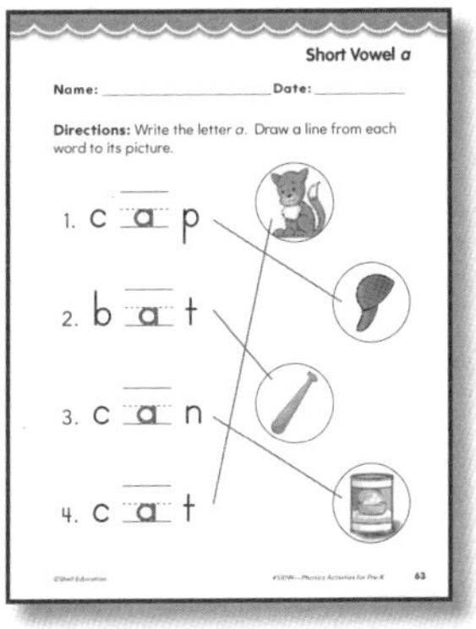
Short Vowel *a*

Name: ______________ Date: ________

Directions: Write the letter *a*. Draw a line from each word to its picture.

1. c a p
2. b a t
3. c a n
4. c a t

page 67

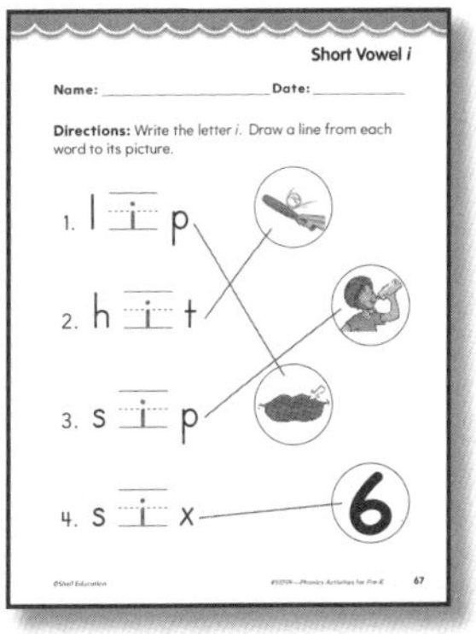
Short Vowel *i*

Name: ______________ Date: ________

Directions: Write the letter *i*. Draw a line from each word to its picture.

1. l i p
2. h i t
3. s i p
4. s i x

page 60

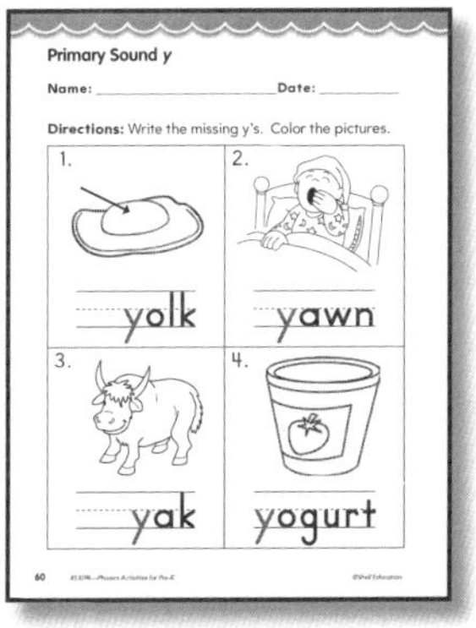
Primary Sound *y*

Name: ______________ Date: ________

Directions: Write the missing y's. Color the pictures.

1. yolk
2. yawn
3. yak
4. yogurt

page 64

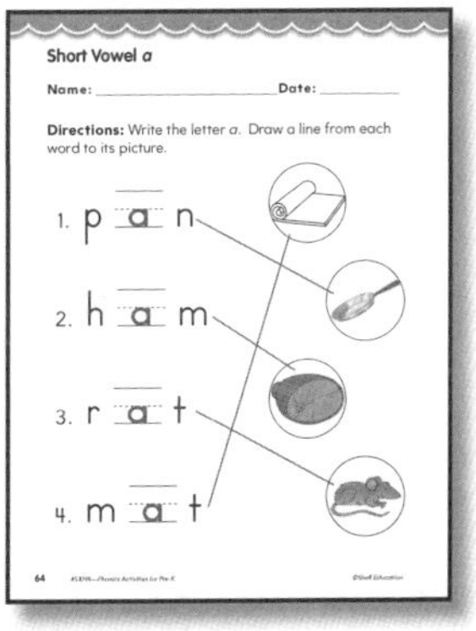
Short Vowel *a*

Name: ______________ Date: ________

Directions: Write the letter *a*. Draw a line from each word to its picture.

1. p a n
2. h a m
3. r a t
4. m a t

page 68

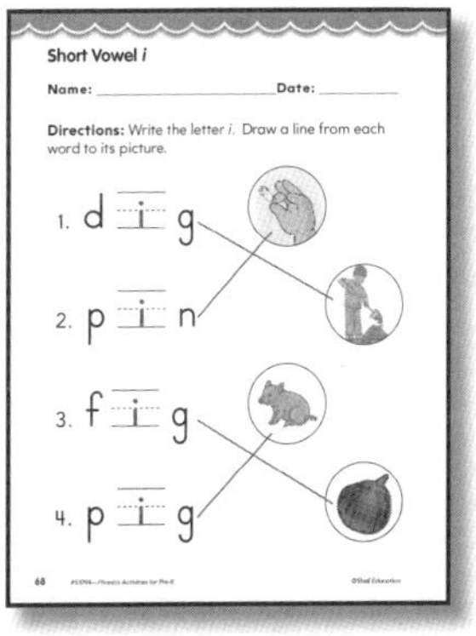
Short Vowel *i*

Name: ______________ Date: ________

Directions: Write the letter *i*. Draw a line from each word to its picture.

1. d i g
2. p i n
3. f i g
4. p i g

page 61

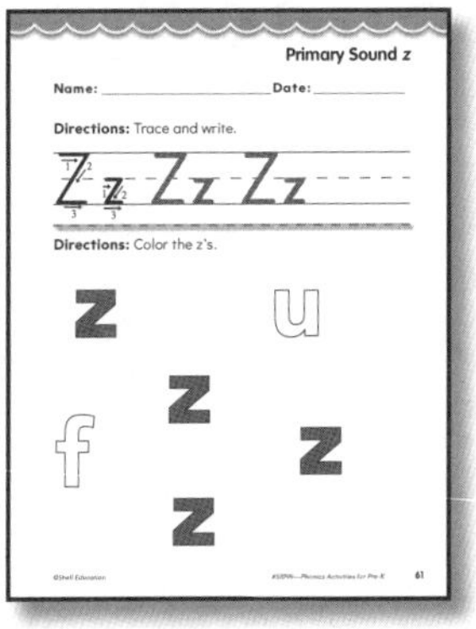
Primary Sound *z*

Name: ______________ Date: ________

Directions: Trace and write.

Zz Zz Zz

Directions: Color the z's.

z u z f z z

page 65

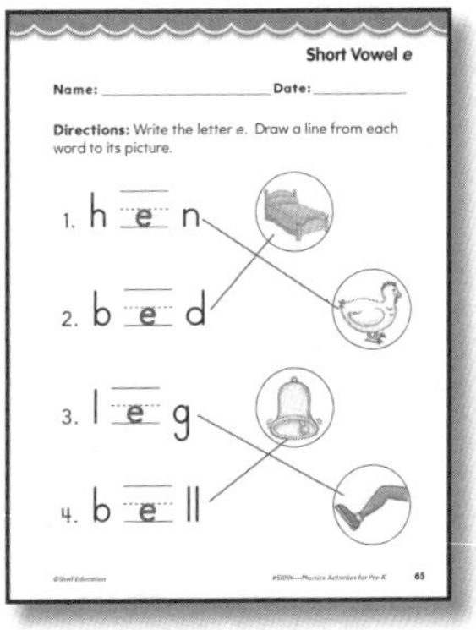
Short Vowel *e*

Name: ______________ Date: ________

Directions: Write the letter *e*. Draw a line from each word to its picture.

1. h e n
2. b e d
3. l e g
4. b e ll

page 69

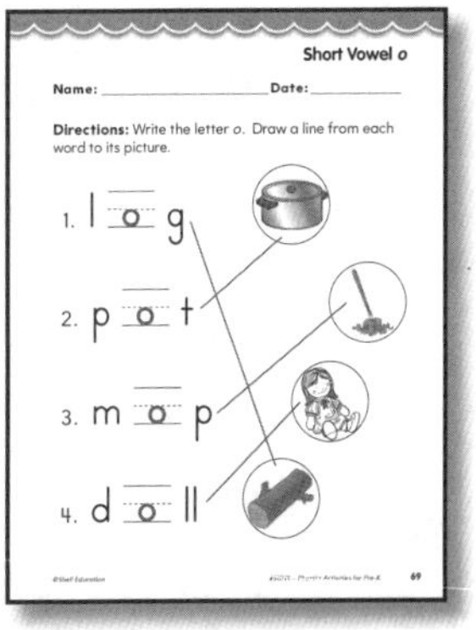
Short Vowel *o*

Name: ______________ Date: ________

Directions: Write the letter *o*. Draw a line from each word to its picture.

1. l o g
2. p o t
3. m o p
4. d o ll

page 62

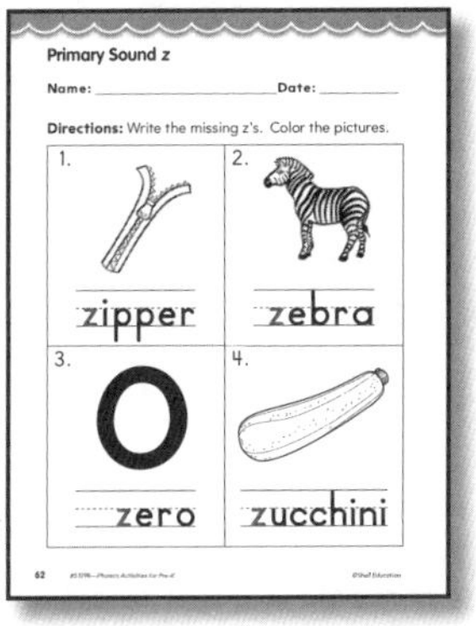
Primary Sound *z*

Name: ______________ Date: ________

Directions: Write the missing z's. Color the pictures.

1. zipper
2. zebra
3. zero
4. zucchini

page 66

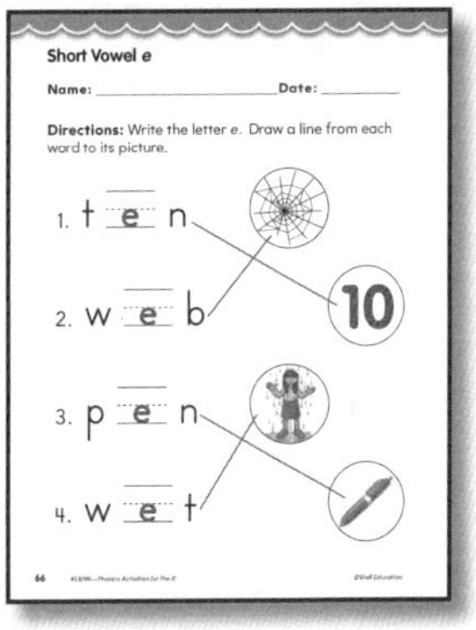
Short Vowel *e*

Name: ______________ Date: ________

Directions: Write the letter *e*. Draw a line from each word to its picture.

1. t e n
2. w e b
3. p e n
4. w e t

page 70

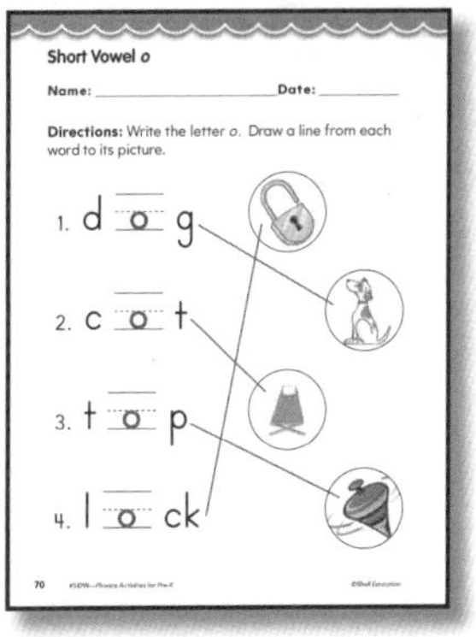
Short Vowel *o*

Name: ______________ Date: ________

Directions: Write the letter *o*. Draw a line from each word to its picture.

1. d o g
2. c o t
3. t o p
4. l o ck

Answer Key *(cont.)*

page 71

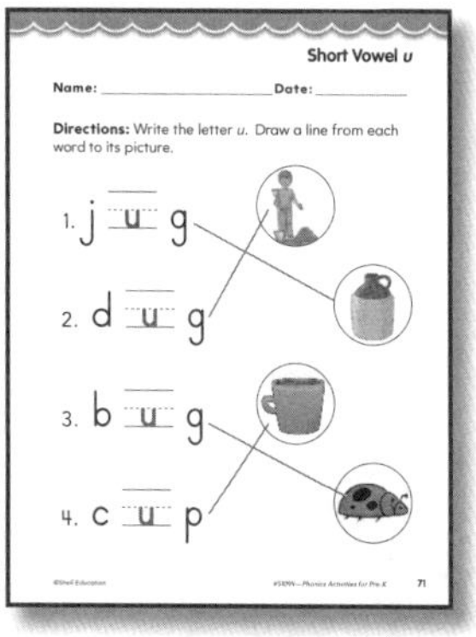
Short Vowel *u*

Name: ____________ Date: ________

Directions: Write the letter *u*. Draw a line from each word to its picture.

1. j u g
2. d u g
3. b u g
4. c u p

page 75

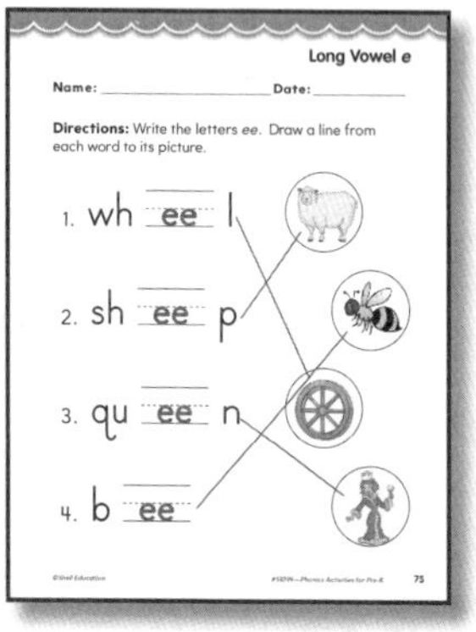
Long Vowel *e*

Name: ____________ Date: ________

Directions: Write the letters *ee*. Draw a line from each word to its picture.

1. wh ee l
2. sh ee p
3. qu ee n
4. b ee

page 79

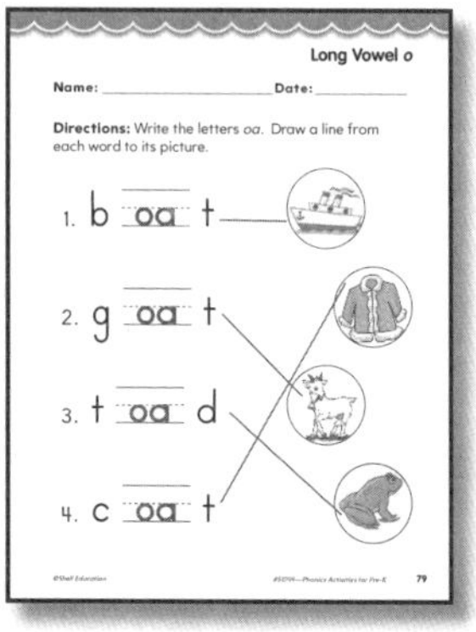
Long Vowel *o*

Name: ____________ Date: ________

Directions: Write the letters *oa*. Draw a line from each word to its picture.

1. b oa t
2. g oa t
3. t oa d
4. c oa t

page 72

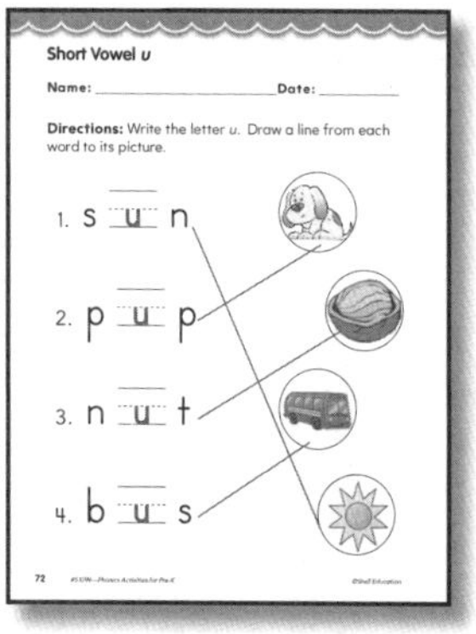
Short Vowel *u*

Name: ____________ Date: ________

Directions: Write the letter *u*. Draw a line from each word to its picture.

1. s u n
2. p u p
3. n u t
4. b u s

page 76

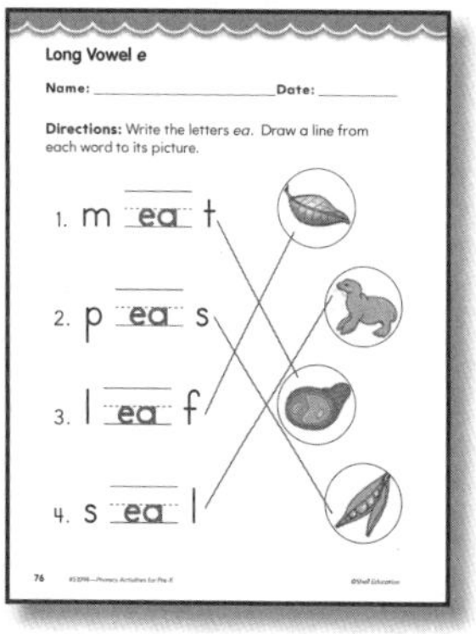
Long Vowel *e*

Name: ____________ Date: ________

Directions: Write the letters *ea*. Draw a line from each word to its picture.

1. m ea t
2. p ea s
3. l ea f
4. s ea l

page 80

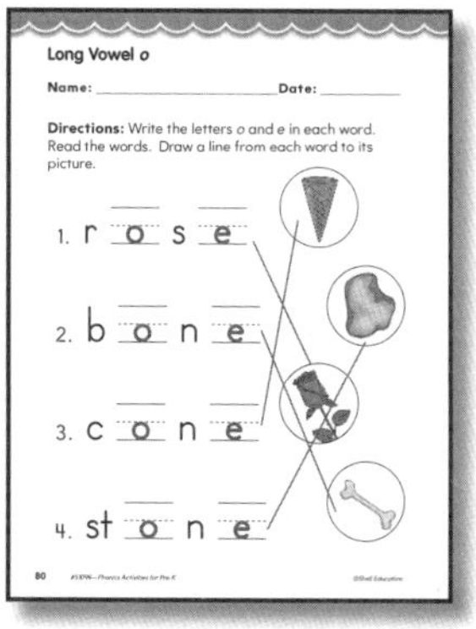
Long Vowel *o*

Name: ____________ Date: ________

Directions: Write the letters *o* and *e* in each word. Read the words. Draw a line from each word to its picture.

1. r o s e
2. b o n e
3. c o n e
4. st o n e

page 73

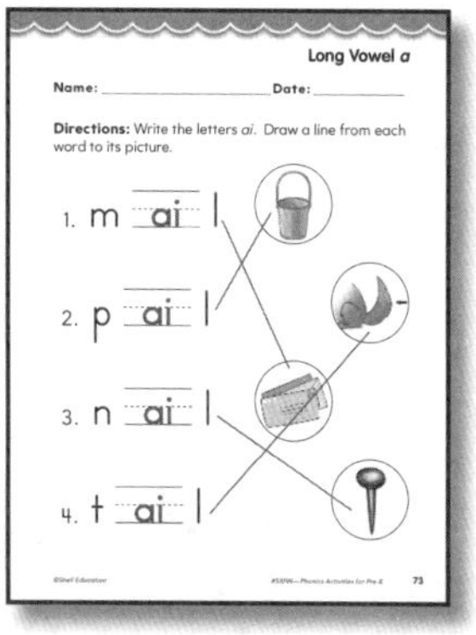
Long Vowel *a*

Name: ____________ Date: ________

Directions: Write the letters *ai*. Draw a line from each word to its picture.

1. m ai l
2. p ai l
3. n ai l
4. t ai l

page 77

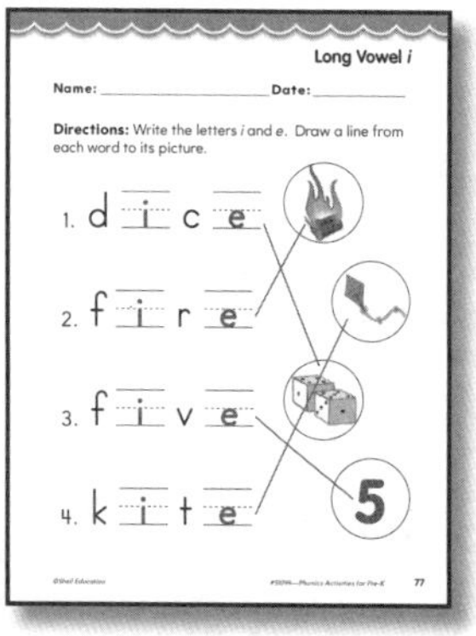
Long Vowel *i*

Name: ____________ Date: ________

Directions: Write the letters *i* and *e*. Draw a line from each word to its picture.

1. d i c e
2. f i r e
3. f i v e
4. k i t e

page 81

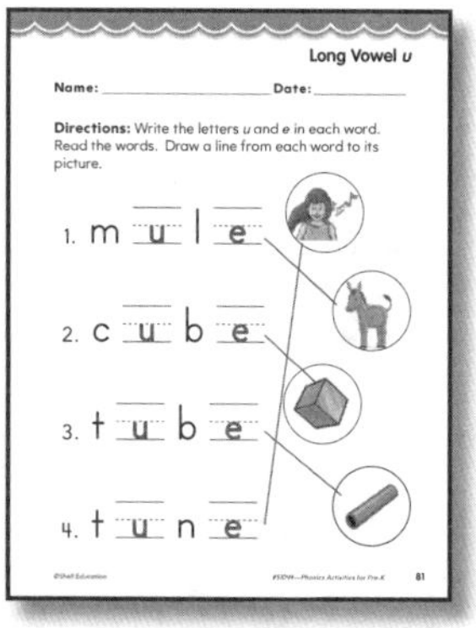
Long Vowel *u*

Name: ____________ Date: ________

Directions: Write the letters *u* and *e* in each word. Read the words. Draw a line from each word to its picture.

1. m u l e
2. c u b e
3. t u b e
4. t u n e

page 74

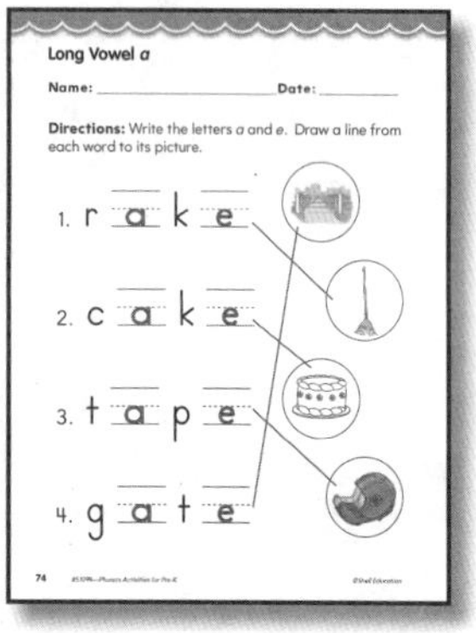
Long Vowel *a*

Name: ____________ Date: ________

Directions: Write the letters *a* and *e*. Draw a line from each word to its picture.

1. r a k e
2. c a k e
3. t a p e
4. g a t e

page 78

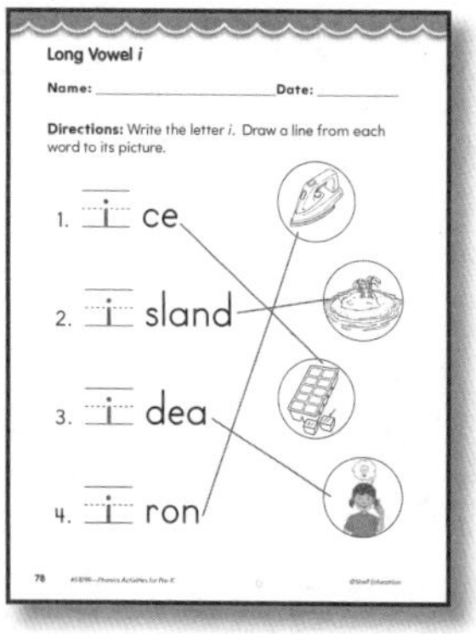
Long Vowel *i*

Name: ____________ Date: ________

Directions: Write the letter *i*. Draw a line from each word to its picture.

1. i ce
2. i sland
3. i dea
4. i ron

page 82

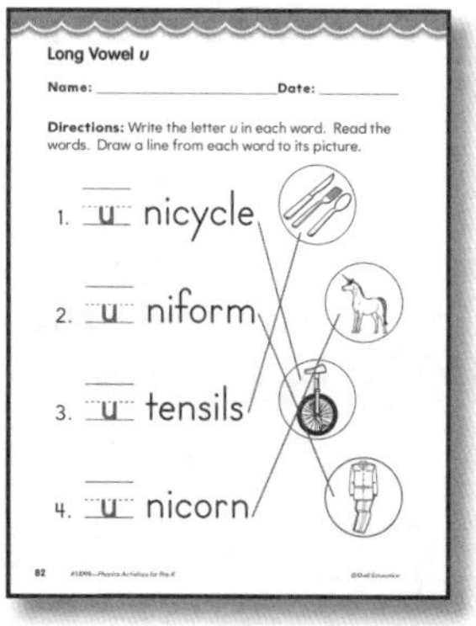
Long Vowel *u*

Name: ____________ Date: ________

Directions: Write the letter *u* in each word. Read the words. Draw a line from each word to its picture.

1. u nicycle
2. u niform
3. u tensils
4. u nicorn

Answer Key *(cont.)*

page 83

page 86

page 84

page 87

page 85

Contents of the Digital Resource CD

Page	Filename
11	page11.pdf
12	page12.pdf
13	page13.pdf
14	page14.pdf
15	page15.pdf
16	page16.pdf
17	page17.pdf
18	page18.pdf
19	page19.pdf
20	page20.pdf
21	page21.pdf
22	page22.pdf
23	page23.pdf
24	page24.pdf
25	page25.pdf
26	page26.pdf
27	page27.pdf
28	page28.pdf
29	page29.pdf
30	page30.pdf
31	page31.pdf
32	page32.pdf
33	page33.pdf
34	page34.pdf
35	page35.pdf
36	page36.pdf
37	page37.pdf
38	page38.pdf
39	page39.pdf
40	page40.pdf
41	page41.pdf
42	page42.pdf
43	page43.pdf
44	page44.pdf
45	page45.pdf
46	page46.pdf
47	page47.pdf
48	page48.pdf
49	page49.pdf
50	page50.pdf

Page	Filename
51	page51.pdf
52	page52.pdf
53	page53.pdf
54	page54.pdf
55	page55.pdf
56	page56.pdf
57	page57.pdf
58	page58.pdf
59	page59.pdf
60	page60.pdf
61	page61.pdf
62	page62.pdf
63	page63.pdf
64	page64.pdf
65	page65.pdf
66	page66.pdf
67	page67.pdf
68	page68.pdf
69	page69.pdf
70	page70.pdf
71	page71.pdf
72	page72.pdf
73	page73.pdf
74	page74.pdf
75	page75.pdf
76	page76.pdf
77	page77.pdf
78	page78.pdf
79	page79.pdf
80	page80.pdf
81	page81.pdf
82	page82.pdf
83	page83.pdf
84	page84.pdf
85	page85.pdf
86	page86.pdf
87	page87.pdf